JB JOSSEY-BASS™
A Wiley Brand

T0327704

Nurturing New Volunteers

86 Ways to Build Long-term Relationships With New Recruits

Scott C. Stevenson, Editor

WILEY

Nurturing New Volunteers

86 Ways to Build Long-term Relationships With New Recruits

Published by

Stevenson, Inc.

P.O. Box 4528 • Sioux City, Iowa • 51104
Phone 712.239.3010 • Fax 712.239.2166

www.stevensoninc.com

Nurturing New Volunteers

86 Ways to Build Long-term Relationships With New Recruits

Table of Contents

Nurturing New Volunteers

86 Ways to Build Long-term Relationships With New Recruits

Table of Contents

Nurturing New Volunteers

86 Ways to Build Long-term Relationships With New Recruits

1. Communicate With Volunteers in Multiple Ways

How do you communicate with your volunteers? Oftentimes you can stay in touch more effectively and meaningfully by using multiple communication methods. Rely on these and other methods for staying close to your volunteers:

E-mail — More and more individuals are relying on e-mail as a way to communicate. It's instantaneous and can be used for both individual and group messages.

Social networking — Increasing numbers of people first turn to Facebook, LinkedIn, My Space and other social networking technologies as a way to find out what's happening and share information.

Personal correspondence — There's nothing more meaningful than a brief note to let an individual know he/she is in your thoughts.

Phone and conference calls — Reserve a minimum number of daily or weekly phone calls to update volunteers or board members. For business that involves groups of busy volunteers — particularly those at a distance — conference calls can be an effective way to communicate. And don't overlook cell phone texting as one other alternative with some.

One-on-one visits — These more time-consuming meetings not only allow for a more thorough discussion of issues, but also provide a chance to learn more about the person with whom you're meeting.

Reports at meetings — A 10-minute appearance at a volunteer meeting lets volunteers know you're aware of their important contributions and allows you to share pertinent information as well.

Memos and newsletters — Regular print communications ensure that you can convey important information to everyone on your list and keep the name and mission of your organization in front of volunteers and board members.

2. Five Ways to Recognize and Nurture Your Volunteers

Volunteers are an invaluable resource for your nonprofit, so be sure to offer recognition to your group of volunteers each and every day. Use this list of tips to help recognition become a priority in your nonprofit:

1. **Honor preferences.** Start the relationship with each volunteer with a clear understanding of his/her areas of interest, and work diligently not to veer from it. A content, well-placed volunteer is likely to stick around long-term.

2. **Connect education and career skills with a volunteer's role.** To further the point above, use relevant assessment tools to easily gauge a volunteer's skill set and determine how those skills can best be used to serve your organization.

3. **Continue to challenge them.** Set in place a standard review process, so volunteers can voice their need for growth.

4. **Remain upbeat and positive.** Never, under any circumstances, complain to or in front of volunteers. Keep the environment positive and cheerful, and your volunteers will continue to come back to pitch in time after time.

5. **Nurture their goals.** Does your volunteer want more responsibility to gain important work skills or further their education in the nonprofit sector? Learn more about your volunteers' motivations by asking open-ended questions and sending pointed volunteer surveys.

There are multiple reasons for communicating with volunteers in multiple ways:

a) They may respond to one method over another.

b) Your communications will be perceived as less monotonous if they arrive in varied formats.

c) Recipients are more likely to pay attention and comprehend your messages if they are delivered in multiple ways.

Although volunteers require varying levels of affirmation, it's particularly wise to recognize new recruits' contributions.

3. Boost Retention With the Help of Mentors

Aligning volunteers with mentors from within your organization and the community can create a stronger sense of mission and boost volunteer retention. To create volunteer-mentor relationships:

✓ Ask leaders from corporations that sponsor your events or support your mission to identify mentors within their ranks who can be resources to your volunteers. Does this company have a professional event planner? If so, ask to align that professional with your special events volunteers to create a stronger support network.

✓ Identify leaders within your nonprofit to act as volunteer mentors. Could a board member with specific professional skills lead a team of volunteers or mentor a single volunteer? Ask a board member who has professional fundraising skills to help oversee your fundraising volunteers, guiding them to stretch their skills.

✓ Cooperate with a fellow nonprofit organization by sharing skilled mentors. Does another nonprofit have an extraordinary professional speaker? Is this person willing to mentor outreach volunteers within your nonprofit and help them polish their skills? Offer this nonprofit the same mentorship possibilities from your organization's leaders.

Seasoned volunteers can speed up the learning process for new volunteers, and mentoring can be a very enriching experienced for those doing the teaching and training.

4. No Volunteer Is the Same as Any Other

If you have a group of volunteers, it's pretty safe to bet they have different interests and personalities. So why treat them all the same when it comes to saying thanks?

The Madison Senior Center (Madison, WI) relies on its nearly 300 volunteers to help keep the center going. And that's why in 2008 the center developed a unique volunteer recognition program. "Since no volunteer has the same experience, interests or skill set (as any other), neither is the way each prefers to be recognized. So we changed our approach from offering one recognition dinner per year to creating a set of different activities and events that might appeal to different volunteer tastes," says Rick Orton, volunteer coordinator at the Madison Senior Center.

The special events the volunteers at the senior center are invited to include the following:

- Annual Recognition Breakfast
- Summer Picnic
- Festival of Wreaths Reception
- Antique & Collectibles Appraisal Fair
- Fall Rendezvous/Lunch
- Classic English Tea

Recognize the individuality of your new volunteers. Each brings a different set of skills and talents to your organization.

This list of special events is updated yearly and printed on a card mailed with a thank-you note to each volunteer every February. Orton says although some of their volunteers do not need or want recognition, others really appreciate and take advantage of the activities or events offered.

But special events aren't the only ways the volunteer recognition program at the senior center says thanks. The program also includes:

- Sending birthday cards to all volunteers.
- Offering low-cost vouchers for tickets to select community performing arts events on a quarterly basis.
- Offering and depositing credits for volunteer hours served at the senior center by community TimeBank members. (TimeBank is a program offered in several communities as a way for volunteers to share their skills and talents.)
- Publishing a Volunteer Spotlight article featuring a different volunteer each month in the agency newsletter.
- Offering a personal, cheery "thank you" to volunteers at every chance available.

Source: Rick Orton, Volunteer Coordinator, Madison Senior Center, Madison, WI.
E-mail: rorton@cityofmadison.com

5. Keep Volunteer Inertia at Bay

Without flexibility built into your volunteer program, your volunteers can feel their duties are becoming stagnant, and they may consider looking for opportunities elsewhere. Don't let that happen.

Here are a few ideas to keep your volunteers excited about and engaged with your organization:

Continue to take actions designed to keep your volunteers motivated — even your new recruits.

✓ **Build latitude into guidelines and policies.** Yes, volunteers need to have boundaries. They also need the opportunity to be creative, and, in some cases, to fail. They need to know that you have faith in them either way.

✓ **Ask their opinions.** Whether with a well-timed survey, focus group or one-on-one conversations, ask for volunteers' opinions and ideas. Listen to your volunteers, and you may be surprised by what you hear.

✓ **Revisit their commitment with them.** Persons may sign up to do one thing for your organization, but eventually realize they'd like to do something else or their life circumstances have changed. Check in with them from time to time to see if they still feel well-matched.

✓ **Ask questions.** Specifically, ask what you can do to help them in their role, and then follow through with appropriate actions.

6. Take Volunteer Care Seriously

At Hope HealthCare Services (Fort Myers, FL), a number of volunteers spend time with people who are terminally ill. With this kind of often-stressful activity, volunteers could be at risk of a serious condition known as compassion fatigue.

Proactive and preventative steps will help to avoid "compassion fatigue" among your volunteers.

Hope HealthCare Services is supported by more than 1,000 volunteers. During the organization's 30-year history, they have experienced no problems with volunteer compassion fatigue or burnout, says Samira K. Beckwith, president and CEO. She attributes that to proactive and preventative steps they take.

"We are very active in showing our volunteers the same compassion that we show to those in our care," says Beckwith. "Their well-being is our priority."

Here, Beckwith shares ways Hope HealthCare Services combats compassion fatigue before it becomes an issue:

✓ "Our volunteer specialists and staff members closely monitor volunteer activities through progress notes, phone calls and mentor calls," she says. "This is one way of identifying and alleviating any stress in its earliest stages."

✓ Volunteers are told they can say no to a request from Hope at any time. By monitoring their activities, we try to ensure they are not put in a position in which they will have to say no.

✓ After a stressful assignment, volunteers are encouraged to take time off for as long as they need it.

✓ Continuing education classes, such as How to Deal with Stress, are offered as a preventative measure.

✓ Volunteers are encouraged to have fun, through ice cream socials, coffee hour, brown bag lunches and our annual volunteer appreciation event. These are ways of demonstrating that we care and it facilitates socialization, which greatly contributes to their satisfaction as a volunteer.

✓ We show appreciation for what they do, so volunteers know they make a difference, which she says is "the best way to help them avoid compassion fatigue."

Source: Samira K. Beckwith, President and CEO, Hope HealthCare Services, Fort Myers, FL.

7. Varying Teaching Styles Yields Well-rounded Training

Consider using multiple teaching styles to help volunteers-in-training remain engaged and retain more of the important information they need to assist your organization and its mission.

At Fox Valley Volunteer Hospice (FVVH) of Geneva, IL, persons can expect a variety of teaching styles during their training sessions to help them prepare as thoroughly as possible for the often-emotional tasks involved with volunteering at the organization.

Training as an FVVH bereavement volunteer requires more than 20 hours of intensive training to learn the unique aspects of serving and supporting individuals and families who have experienced the death of a loved one, says Elise C. Wall, manager of volunteer services. Bereavement volunteers not only need to have compassion, Wall says, they need to learn skills in discussing grief, death and dying; to listen without judgment; and to maintain personal boundaries.

Topics covered during training at FVVH include normal adult and children's grief, complicated grief, good communication skills with an emphasis on listening, self-care for both client and volunteer, exploring grief theories and preventing volunteer burnout.

To best cover this extensive list of complicated topics, Wall says, bereavement training includes a variety of teaching and learning styles to assist new volunteers with retention as follows:

The varied teaching styles you use will make learning more enjoyable and fulfilling for new volunteers.

- ❑ **Lectures.** Lectures can offer thorough details and explanations to volunteers, but can also be an area where volunteers can lose information when their minds become inundated or overloaded. Be sure to break lecture training up with frequent breaks as well as small group discussions and role-playing. Create handouts with bullet points of critical information that will allow volunteers the opportunity to review material covered later.

- ❑ **Small group discussions.** Break volunteers into small groups of five or fewer to review accompanying lecture materials or to personalize the information covered based on their experiences as part of the layering process that will help them retain information.

- ❑ **Role-playing.** Offer role-playing to allow volunteers to put the training into action and affirm what they have learned. Ask trainers and seasoned volunteers to role-play with trainees to ensure their understanding of material covered.

- ❑ **On-site training.** Create opportunities for new volunteers to put their new knowledge into play within your organization by offering onsite training. Either pair new volunteers together or ask them to shadow experienced volunteers to witness training techniques in action.

Source: Elise C. Wall, Manager of Volunteer Services, Fox Valley Volunteer Hospice, Geneva, IL.
E-mail: ewall@fvvh.org

Teach Effective Listening

A key component to offering effective support to clients facing the death of a loved one is the art of effective listening. In bereavement training, volunteers at the Fox Valley Volunteer Hospice (Geneva, IL) learn to listen effectively.

Elise C. Wall, manager of volunteer services, shares techniques they teach, which can also help your volunteers to become more effective listeners:

- ✓ Listening with the intent to understand rather than with the intent to respond.
- ✓ Using open body language (e.g., arms and legs uncrossed).
- ✓ Maintaining eye contact with the client.
- ✓ Staying focused on the client, not allowing the mind to wander.
- ✓ Affirming the client's words with a nod.
- ✓ Being comfortable with silence, allowing the client to process his/her thoughts.
- ✓ Avoiding jumping to conclusions.

8. Organize Projects for Successful Completion

Have you carefully organized a project for newly-appointed volunteers, only to return and find that it has been done incorrectly? The fault may be insufficient instruction. As a manager, it's your job to get volunteers off to a successful start and empower them to complete the task.

The following planning steps will help get your crew off to a positive start and allow you to focus your time and energy on other areas of responsibility:

1. **Review the project with the volunteers.** Provide background, review instructions and justify the deadline, so they understand the full scope of the project.

2. **Detail instructions in writing.** Even if instructions appear elementary to you, volunteers do not have your background or perspective.

3. **Provide a completion deadline.** This helps volunteers prioritize tasks and recognize if more help is needed.

4. **Assign a leader.** If you are not supervising the project, make sure one volunteer has leadership authority to organize the crew, make decisions and resolve problems.

5. **Be present at the kickoff.** You can spot problems and make corrections immediately, avoiding the embarrassment of asking volunteers to undo or redo a project.

6. **Make it fun.** Mundane projects get lots of support if people's social needs are met. Offer refreshments, snacks, music, opportunities to work in teams and generous praise.

The time taken on the front end of a volunteer project will help to ensure its successful completion.

It's important new volunteers learn to complete assignments properly. These simple steps will help to ensure that happens.

9. Integrate Risk Management Measures in Volunteer Handbook

When creating a volunteer handbook, don't forget to incorporate important risk management measures as a guide for your volunteers. Adding important risk management details will arm your volunteers with information on boundaries that should not be crossed and safeguard your nonprofit. Consider adding the following important risk management measures to protect your volunteers:

- As a volunteer, you must secure your own boundaries when working with a client or in the field. If you are feeling uncertain about a situation, ask before you act. Use your own best judgment, and don't be afraid to ask for clarification or help from your volunteer manager.

- Always travel with a fellow volunteer when working off-site.

- When working with children or clients who are members of the opposite sex, always be in the presence of another adult and/or volunteer team member.

- Do not share personal contact information with clients.

- Keep any information pertaining to clients confidential, including full names and medical conditions. There are confidentiality laws that pertain to certain information. Outline these in the volunteer manual.

- If you have any concerns regarding the safety or well-being of a client, please share this information with the service site supervisor.

- Be aware that you can decline to perform a task when you feel the request is inappropriate, beyond your skill level or training level or if you perceive a situation to be unsafe physically or emotionally.

Be sure your handbook addresses key risk management issues you'll want your new volunteers to be fully aware of as they begin their jobs.

10. Refresh Your Volunteer Program With New Incentives

Does your volunteer program need a pick-me-up and new recruits? Consider adding new incentives that will refresh your volunteer program to draw new volunteers and retain your experienced group of volunteers.

Implement new incentives associated with volunteer tasks or milestones in the following ways:

- Offer a welcome package when a new volunteer signs a volunteer agreement after an initial introductory phase. For example, after one month of service, ask volunteers to sign a volunteer agreement outlining their commitment and hours of planned service, then hand out the welcome package could containing a T-shirt, name badge and a water bottle with your nonprofit's logo on it.

- After a marked number of hours or years served, provide tickets to your premium events as a volunteer incentive, so volunteers can attend as a guest.

- Partner with a local convenience store to offer gas gift cards for volunteers who contribute use of their cars as part of their volunteer service.

- Work with a local business or bank to feature volunteers on marquees when they've contributed an allotted number of service hours. Local banks can become significant partners when promoting community volunteerism and offering volunteer incentives that feature the bank's logo.

- Provide incentives by way of a savings bond that equates to the number of hours of service. For example, when a volunteer hits 100 hours of service, award them with a $100 savings bond. Savings bonds can be purchased for significantly less than the face value of the bond. Find out more at www.treasurydirect.gov.

Periodic incentives will help to keep new volunteers engaged and coming back for more.

11. To Understand Your Volunteers, Walk in Their Shoes

Want to know what your volunteers think and feel about their service? Volunteer for a day or two alongside them. Stay alert throughout this process, and you will discover information that will improve volunteers' experiences and make you a better volunteer manager.

You may recognize challenges, holes in training, frustrations with insufficient resources, how paid staff perceive volunteers, or clues to volunteer retention. In addition, you will come to understand volunteers' motivations, recognize their true contributions, glimpse hidden talents and understand the role volunteering plays in their lives.

Here are examples of improvements made by working alongside volunteers:

1. One volunteer manager noticed her volunteers' highest need was social interaction, which led to restructuring assignments so two or more people were assigned to a task.

2. Another manager discovered volunteers wanted more physical activity, so she created a messenger service. The opportunity to retrieve files, deliver mail and run errands led to friendly competition for the position. Volunteers wore pedometers and recorded mileage rather than compiling service hours.

3. Yet another manager learned that volunteers did not understand corporate acronyms and lingo, and created a pocket-sized vocabulary pamphlet that solved the problem.

> ### Rules to Remember
> - Remember the rule of reciprocation. When someone carries out an act of kindness towards you, it's natural to want to return the favor. Do something nice for those around you every day.

By stepping down from your administrative role to serve alongside volunteers, you will earn their respect and just may find them sharing insights and solutions to problems.

12. Inject Spur-of-the-Moment Activities Into Work Experience

Sometimes the most appreciated activities are those that take place spontaneously — or at least seem to in the minds of your volunteers.

As you look for ways to thank your volunteers and keep them excited about their work, make a point to occasionally interject a surprise activity to break up an otherwise mundane work experience, or to reward them for a job well done.

Here are some ideas to add to your secret menu of spur-of-the-moment activities:

It never hurts to throw in a surprise now and then to keep work from becoming too mundane.

- Take your volunteers to an afternoon movie.
- Phone volunteers' families to meet you and your volunteers for a surprise picnic.
- Organize a softball game or some other recreational activity with your volunteers.
- Line up a small music ensemble to walk into your volunteers' work area and serenade them.
- Invite those served by your organization (e.g., youth, students, patients) to stage a program for your volunteers.
- Have a meal or gourmet dessert delivered.
- For a phonathon, have a massage therapist give shoulder massages.

Your surprise celebrations don't need to be elaborate to be appreciated. But they do need to happen from time to time.

13. Have Volunteers Sign a Code of Conduct

Content not available in this edition

Content not available in this edition

The way volunteers behave while serving your organization in public has a big impact on how the organization is perceived. Having volunteers sign a code of conduct agreement can protect you legally and set a precedent that excellent performance is expected. Blanche Hudon, Director of Volunteer Services for the Central North Carolina Chapter of the American Red Cross, answers the following questions about codes of conduct:

When do volunteers sign the code of conduct, and how do you reinforce good behavior?

"All volunteers attend an orientation. During this time we clarify expectations, provide training, answer questions and have them sign the code of conduct. You can't just assume that signing a piece of paper will cause good behavior, so training is important."

Do you use the same code of conduct for volunteers and employees, or are they different?

"The same code of conduct is used for both staff and volunteers. It is a national policy implemented by all local chapters. Using the same policy shows volunteers how important their service is, and sets a high standard for behavior."

What topics does the code of conduct cover?

"It is a thorough document that covers prohibited behaviors such as using the name and logo of American Red Cross for personal use, accepting or seeking financial advantage, (breaching) confidentiality, promoting politics or religious matters not in conformity with the official position of American Red Cross, retaliation, and acting in any manner not in the best interest of American Red Cross."

Source: Blanche Hudon, Director of Volunteer Services, American Red Cross, Central North Carolina Chapter, Durham, NC. E-mail: hudonb@usa.redcross.org

14. Intense Training Precedes Zoo Volunteer Assignments

At the Prospect Park Zoo (Brooklyn, NY), 36 education docents serve as volunteer educators, offering a new, unique element to members as well as to the volunteer program.

Due to the more involved nature of becoming an education docent, the training requirements are more intense for this volunteer group. Those persons who are accepted into the program can expect to attend weekly training sessions for approximately four months. These sessions cover topics such as conservation, biology and informal learning. Trained docents can then begin to offer member tours, manage discovery stations and help at special events.

Docent trainees are required to take a series of 10 to 12 classes, which include a volunteer basics class covering the history of the Prospect Park Zoo and the Wildlife Conservation Society; on-site volunteering; handling animal contact areas such as the zoo's barn, wallaby/kangaroo exhibit, and walk-through aviary; zoo safety; and interacting with the public.

Key into your new volunteers, especially when the training requirements are intense.

Docents then go on to take classes in interpretation, including exhibit and biofact interpretation, conservation, animal chats and tour leading, and the final classes are in animal handling, which include weekly written protocol tests, handling practice, plus a final live animal encounter demonstration to pass.

"As for commitment, education docents are required to complete 120 hours per year, and are asked to volunteer on a regular schedule. Most volunteer one-half day per week, but many docents do much more," says Debbie Dieneman Keim, coordinator of volunteers. "We also offer docent meetings about eight to nine times per year, which include presentations from our director, the animal department, and education department, or field trips to other facilities. Animal handlers are required to attend two animal handling meetings per year and submit a negative TB test result before training and every year after that to maintain their handling status."

Dieneman Keim offers the following tips for developing a successful education docents or similar program at your nonprofit:

✓ **Make these volunteers feel needed.** "Our zoo could truly not function without our volunteers," she says. "We have areas in the zoo that must be monitored at all times — animal contact areas, our Animals in Art exhibit and our Discovery Center and our volunteers know we need them."

✓ **Listen to their ideas and use their talents.** "Many of our volunteers have done research for our animal fact sheets, created themed biofact carts, and created games or craft projects for special events, or trained to become sea lion feeding narrators."

✓ **Keep in contact and share information.** "Although we do not have a formal newsletter," she says, "I try to reach out to everyone with e-mail updates and chat with them when they are volunteering. Our zoo director, Denise McClean, is often around and willing to chat with volunteers, and that really makes them feel welcome."

✓ **Give them a community.** "Docent meetings bond the volunteer crew together," says Dieneman Keim. "Our animal handlers work in pairs and develop themes for their presentations, which gives them ownership of their programs, and many new friends."

✓ **Celebrate their accomplishments.** Everyone loves praise, parties, and a word of thanks. At the zoo, uniforms are used to reveal the different levels of volunteering; the Discovery Guides and Discovery Center volunteers wear burgundy shirts and docents wear light blue shirts, the same color as the education deptartment's paid staff.

✓ **Have a hook that makes you different.** "Our animal handling program is extremely attractive to potential volunteers," she says. "They develop a real bond with the animals that keeps them coming back. After all, it is really all about the animals!"

Source: Debbie Dieneman Keim, Coordinator of Volunteers, Prospect Park Zoo, Brooklyn, NY.
E-mail: ddieneman@wcs.org

15. Ensure First Volunteer Projects Are a Smashing Success

If you're just getting a volunteer program under way, it's important to build a record of success. To create enthusiasm and momentum, volunteers need to realize a sense of accomplishment. Anything less will have negative consequences.

Don't bite off more than you can chew; select one or two projects that are achievable and do them well. To do that, follow these steps:

1. Enlist a small number of persons who have a track record of past volunteer success.

2. Work with them to select a clearly defined project they can successfully complete.

3. Recognize that these first projects will require more supervisory time.

4. Help participants see the big picture as well as the project's important details.

5. Celebrate your accomplishments and recognize those who made it happen.

6. Use the project's success to attract additional volunteers.

Once your volunteers have had multiple successes, enthusiasm will grow, as will the number of volunteers wanting to join your winning cause.

It's important that whatever new volunteers take on as work assignments or projects, they be successful.

16. Pair Up Volunteers to Maximize Productivity

Many volunteer managers realize the benefits of pairing up volunteers as a way to accomplish certain tasks more effectively.

Paired up, volunteers can often accomplish more than if working individually. They can divide responsibilities, help one another meet deadlines, complement each other's strengths/weaknesses and likes/dislikes and have more fun completing tasks.

Give it a try.

Select a project and assign tasks to volunteer teams of two. Then consider incorporating any or all of the following ideas to maximize productivity from these volunteer duos:

Ever try pairing up volunteers? It has its advantages.

- Create a competition among teams based on different criteria — those who complete projects first (or on time), those who achieve the greatest success, those who are most thorough, etc. — then award prizes accordingly.

- Structure your training sessions so one half of each team gets particular training in one area followed by training in another area for the other team member. In this way you will have trained each member of the paired volunteers in a special area so that together, they can complement one another.

- If your paired volunteers are expected to make calls on others — for instance, on donors or potential sponsors — design a dual script for them. Designate one individual as the lead presenter and the second as the person whose job it is to provide supporting but key information. One person may be charged with doing the asking and the other prepared to answer any questions.

- If your volunteers provide tours, train one to provide more practical information regarding facilities/services, while the other focuses on anecdotal information.

- Pair veterans with rookies to train new recruits and pass the baton.

- Allow spouses and other couples to work as teams — also consider parent/child or even grandparent/grandchild teams.

17. Warm Up to Recruiting Winter-friendly Volunteers

While winter may seem far away, it's not too soon to begin working with your volunteers to plan an event that makes the most of the colder weather.

Duluth's recent two-week long Snowlympics event (Duluth, MN) required the help of hundreds of volunteers. Snowlympics is a two-week festival celebrating Duluth's rich Olympic history and winter activities. More than 2,500 community members participated throughout the festival with the assistance of many volunteers.

Whether you're looking to build on an existing winter event or launch a new one, these tips from Snowlympics Event Coordinator Barbara Weinstein can help you find a substantial number of suitable volunteers for your next winter festival:

1. **Connect with local organizations, such as AmeriCorps, to determine whether they can supply volunteers for your event.** Many Snowlympics events are education-based and require volunteer instructors. With the assistance of True North AmeriCorps members, Snowlympics educational events had a ratio of one instructor for every four participants. "AmeriCorps members were an integral part in developing and implementing several events due to the placement of members in the City of Duluth's Park and Recreation locations," says Weinstein. "Without the leadership and creativity of True North AmeriCorps members the Snowlympics would not be the success it is."

2. **Dovetail with existing cold-weather community events.** Snowlympics staff coordinated efforts within the community with other established annual events. In merging events, Snowlympics organizers were able to retain the annual event volunteers and utilize them for other aspects of the festival.

3. **Look to local clubs and organizations that can provide volunteers with experience in particular events.** Snowlympics organizers worked with local ski and skate clubs to recruit volunteers who could educate community members in skiing and skating as well as showcase their talents at events.

Source: Barbara Weinstein, Event Coordinator, City of Duluth, Duluth, MN.
E-mail: info@fitcityduluth.com

18. Help Fellow Employees Appreciate the Value of Volunteers

Helping colleagues understand the key role volunteers can and do play will strengthen existing volunteer-driven programs and make new initiatives possible.

If your employees begin to recognize the contributions being made by existing volunteers, they may identify new opportunities for volunteer involvement in their own areas of responsibility. In addition, the more all employees recognize the contributions being made by existing volunteers, the more they will join in directing appreciation to them and, as a result, help to retain them.

Decide which of these practical strategies you can implement to help your employees better recognize volunteer contributions:

- Regularly list accomplishments/services of volunteers in your in-house newsletter.
- Make use of a volunteer bulletin board that showcases volunteers and their work.
- Invite a volunteer to speak during an employee meeting, describing his/her duties.
- Create a video — depicting your volunteers in action — that can be checked out by employees and used as a recruitment tool as well.
- Conduct an in-house survey that identifies new volunteer opportunities.

To encourage fellow employees to nurture your new volunteers, help your colleagues understand the value of these "angles in disguise."

19. Present Newcomers With a Welcome Kit

What do new volunteers receive when they join your cause?

How about giving them a welcome kit that shows your appreciation, helps to educate them and demonstrates the high level of expectations you have for them?

Here's a checklist of items that may be appropriate for your new volunteer welcome kit:

❑ Personal notes of welcome and appreciation from those served by your agency.
❑ Letter of appointment and welcome from your organization's board chair.
❑ Directory of staff and volunteer names with phone numbers, and e-mail addresses.
❑ Organizational and/or volunteer structure chart.
❑ Description of programs and services.
❑ Policies and procedures.
❑ Recent issues of your newsletter or agency magazine.
❑ Complimentary tickets to an appropriate event.
❑ An autographed book.

A meaningful welcome kit will make new volunteers' association with your organizaiton more official.

20. Spell Out Expectations to Potential Recruits

It's important to eliminate any surprises when going over expectations with possible volunteers. Leave no room for misunderstandings.

See that the following questions are answered as fully as possible:

1. What are the exact work assignments?
2. How much time will be required on a daily, weekly or monthly basis?
3. Where should/can the assignments be carried out?
4. How many others will be involved in the assignment?
5. What is the time frame?
6. Who among the staff will serve as a resource or supervisor?
7. What type of training/orientation will be required?
8. What will be the outcome of the completed project(s)?
9. What are the volunteer benefits — both tangible and intangible?

21. Make a Good First Impression

Studies show volunteers' first impressions are crucial. In fact, a negative perception of your organization in the first 60 to 90 days can drive new volunteers away.

Take steps to make sure volunteers and potential volunteers are receiving the appropriate image of your organization and the programs you deliver.

Consider these points as you strive to build positive first impressions:

- Review marketing materials to be sure you are putting your best foot forward. Does your newsletter reflect what volunteers do for and with your organization and highlight volunteer successes?
- What impressions do volunteers receive when they walk through your doors? Are staff and other volunteers friendly and helpful? Do you offer an inviting work environment?
- When interviewing would-be volunteers, help them understand their roles and responsibilities up front. Provide a written job description.
- After a volunteer signs a letter of agreement, remain in close contact to answer questions and assist in other ways.
- Finally, be sure volunteers know where, when and how often they will meet, and that they are welcomed as members of the team.

Help to create a positive first impression of your organization and its programs in the eyes of new volunteers.

22. Foster a Meaningful Volunteer Program

Creating and managing meaningful volunteer opportunities for experienced professionals can be difficult, says Lori Halley, a blogger for Wild Apricot (Toronto, Ontario, Canada), a membership management organization.

One organization grappling with this challenge that Halley followed was Volunteer Calgary (Calgary, Alberta, Canada), a group that piloted a project to recruit and involve skilled professionals, with the goal of providing meaning to volunteers and capacity for organizations.

The five most important volunteer management lessons Volunteer Calgary learned from this project were:

- **Essential Strategic Leadership:** The executive director must champion a culture and structure that supports the full integration of highly skilled volunteers.
- **Role and Place of the Manager of Volunteers:** Organizations need a staff volunteer manager who is a member of the management team.
- **Professionally Managed Volunteer Programs:** A professional approach to volunteer management requires a consistent alignment of systems, policies and processes for paid and unpaid staff.
- **Valuing Volunteers:** Volunteers and staff need to understand the value volunteers contribute to the organization. This helps overcome outdated perceptions of "I am/you are just a volunteer."
- **Readiness for an Integrated Human Resource Strategy Approach:** To succeed, this approach needs to be integrated with the organization's strategic plan.

Source: Lori Halley, Wild Apricot Marketing Writer and Blogger, Wild Apricot/Bonasource Inc., Toronto, Ontario, Canada. E-mail: lori@wildapricot.com

> It's critical that the work and assignments you give to volunteers, especially to experienced professionals, be meaningful.

23. Elements of an Effective Volunteer Orientation

Orienting new volunteers to their position and duties, as well as to the organization as a whole, is an important part of any volunteer program. But what should be included in an effective volunteer orientation?

Volunteer training can be approached in different ways, depending on the sector and/or mission of the nonprofit. But most will benefit from distributing a volunteer handbook containing policies and procedures on a range of topics, including the following:

- Disciplinary procedures and consequences
- Grievance policies
- Confidentiality issues
- Appropriate computer usage
- Ethics and moral expectations
- Safety considerations and risks associated with various positions

While orientation is typically viewed as a one-time process carried out at the beginning of a volunteer's tenure, annual refreshers are highly recommended. These not only allow volunteers to recall areas they might have begun to overlook, but also give the organization an opportunity to address and revise any policies that may have become less relevant or out-of-date.

> What should be included in a meaningful volunteer orientation?

24. President's Circle Honors, Retains Volunteers

Creating a President's Circle for volunteers has been one nonprofit's answer to retaining volunteers and honoring the important work they do.

At Foodshare (Bloomfield, CT) — an organization focused on providing assistance to the hungry in greater Hartford — more than 3,000 volunteers are needed annually to manage a vast number of programs.

A volunteer incentive program was implemented to allow these volunteers to earn points through a variety of engagement opportunities, culminating in membership in the prestigious President's Circle, an honor currently held by only 10 individuals and two local businesses.

Groups or individuals who earn four or more points are awarded this honor at an annual luncheon hosted by Gloria McAdam, Foodshare's president and CEO.

John Weedon, volunteer coordinator, offers the following tips for incentivizing your volunteer program by offering a President's Circle point system:

- E-mail eligible volunteers and groups at least once a month with details about the President's Circle club. Within the e-mail, feature one activity eligible for points. For example, in September, the focus was on recruiting potential volunteers among friends and family at Foodshare, and an e-mail notice was generated to alert volunteers to this fact. Because volunteers lead busy lives, it's best not to assume a general e-mail about the club at the beginning of the year will generate rock-star enthusiasm.

- Circulate a list of activities that will earn program points for both individual and group volunteers.

- Contact volunteers and groups that are close to earning four points and offer them a road map with fresh ideas on how to cross the finish line.

- Give the program time to grow. Don't expect the program to be an overnight success; consistent communication and encouragement will result in a successful incentive program over time.

Source: John Weedon, Volunteer Coordinator, Foodshare, Bloomfield, CT. E-mail: jweedon@foodshare.org

Forms such as these describe how points are earned for both individuals and groups using a volunteer incentive point system.

Content not available in this edition

25. Instill Volunteer Confidence

Give volunteers confidence, and they will produce. With that in mind, boost your volunteers' confidence by:

1. Praising them at various times during a project — not only at its completion.
2. Asking them to take on progressively larger assignments.
3. Using them as examples (in their presence) when describing to an audience how to do something.
4. Sending a note of praise about a volunteer to his/her boss.
5. Asking for advice and input on matters not necessarily related to his/her volunteer duties.

Eliminate any doubt in the minds of your new volunteers. Help to instill confidence.

26. Spell Out Volunteer Requirements to Save Time, Funds

Spelling out volunteer requirements from the get-go is an important part of starting volunteers on the best footing. Officials at the UW Medicine, Harborview Medical Center (Seattle, WA) have taken the time to spell out volunteer requirements on their website, detailing information on health screening, security screening, commitment, age, attendance, sign in and sign out, dress code and background checks.

With 450 to 500 volunteers to manage, Monica Singh, MPA, assistant director of volunteer and community services, has found that putting the guidelines front and center is helpful for both the nonprofit and potential volunteers.

"Spelling out the volunteer requirements has been useful in that we have seen an increased rate of accurately completed volunteer applications," says Singh. "The requirements listed are determined by human resources, hospital compliance and privacy policies, process improvement initiatives, state requirements and general experience of working with volunteers."

One advantage of sharing these requirements has been a decrease in the processing time of volunteer applications.

"By clearly stating our requirements up front, volunteer staff spend less time calling volunteer applicants to mail or drop off another required form," she says. "In addition, fewer volunteer applications are mailed back for being incomplete."

This simple step has also had a number of other effects, including:

- Reducing mailing costs.
- Decreasing the number of office phone calls pertaining to specific questions.
- Freeing up volunteer services staff to work on other tasks and programs.
- Reducing misunderstandings and communication errors about basic applicant requirements.
- Speeding up application processing time, allowing volunteers to be interviewed more quickly and efficiently.

Source: Monica Singh, MPA, Assistant Director Volunteer and Community Services, UW Medicine, Harborview Medical Center, Seattle, WA. E-mail: ms5@u.washington.edu

---

How to Create an Effective Volunteer Requirements List

Monica Singh, MPA, assistant director of volunteer and community services at UW Medicine, Harborview Medical Center (Seattle, WA), shares tips for creating the most effective list of volunteer requirements:

- Hold a brainstorming session with your volunteer services employees. Include key hospital staff who have a vested interest in creating a volunteer program that supports the hospital's HR policies and compliance standards.

- As a team, make a list of all the requirements that a volunteer applicant must meet before he/she can start volunteering in the organization.

- Get input from all your key stakeholders, so they can provide their perspective and represent the organization's varied interests.

---

27. Six Ways to Keep Your Volunteers Coming Back

It sounds cliché, but volunteers really are the heart of most nonprofit organizations. Without them, work would simply not get done. To show how much you appreciate them:

1. **Thank the volunteer's family.** When people volunteer for you, they are not just giving their time; they are also giving up time they could be spending with their family. Roger Carr, nonprofit blogger, says sending a thank-you note to spouses and/or children is a nice way to acknowledge that.

2. **Send a recognition letter to the volunteer's employer.** Doing so, Carr says, lets employers know about great things their employees do on their own time.

3. **Crunch numbers.** As a regular part of your volunteer recognition program, calculate the value of the time each volunteer has given that year. Simply multiply the number of hours served by current minimum wage and share that number with them. It can be a real eye opener for you too, letting you know how much you saved by having a volunteer do work for you rather than hiring it out.

4. **Include them.** Let your volunteers in on classes, events or meetings your organization offers to which they might not normally have access. Offer volunteers free or discounted memberships. Give volunteers complimentary tickets to your events.

5. **Take it online.** Create an online donor wall. Recognize a volunteer of the month via social media such as Twitter or Facebook.

6. **Nominate them.** Consider nominating some volunteers for Presidential Service Awards or statewide or community-wide honors.

Source: Roger Carr, Nonprofit Blogger, www.everydaygivingblog.com, Fredericksburg, VA. E-mail: roger@everdaygiving.com

It's good to remember that anyone willing to volunteer has lots of choices as to where that will occur. That's why what you do needs to stand out among other volunteer organizations.

28. Prepare Staff Before Placing Volunteers

Once staff members request volunteer assistance and you supply needed personnel, do staff know what to do at that point? When new volunteers show up, will the staff member in charge support them in a way consistent with your expectations?

If you are going to supply departments with needed volunteers, it's important they accommodate those unpaid helpers in a professional manner. Here's how to help:

1. Insist that any personnel desiring volunteer assistance first participate in a brief workshop designed to show the dos and don'ts of working with volunteers.

2. When requests are made for volunteer assistance — and such requests should be encouraged — have a process in place that allows you to get all of the needed facts before enlisting help: How many volunteers will be required? What will they be expected to do? Who will be on hand to assist them or answer questions? What is the time frame of the assigned task(s)? Are there any special qualifications?

3. If possible, check up on the volunteers to be sure everything is going as expected. In addition, be sure they know they can come to you if they have a problem or question that is not being addressed by the department for which they are working.

4. Have a system in place that allows you to survey both volunteers and staff as part of your evaluation of the completed project. Knowing perceptions of both staff and volunteers enables you to make needed improvements.

Help fellow employees understand their role in supporting and nurturing your volunteers.

29. Key Into What Motivates Volunteers to Match Them to Tasks

When you get a new volunteer, do you simply assign the person to the next available task, hand him/her a name tag and move on to your next duty?

Hold on — taking a few more minutes to get to know not just when your volunteer is available, but why he/she is choosing to be available, can result in a much more satisfying partnership for both you and the volunteer.

When enlisting volunteers and matching them with tasks, recognize the distinct difference between skills and likes. A volunteer may be skilled at something but would much prefer to do something else. Just because an attorney is skilled in legal matters, for example, doesn't mean she wants volunteer assignments related to her profession. She may, in fact, prefer a diversion from her daily routine.

> Even if you only have a limited number of available assignments for new volunteers, get a sense of what they enjoy and dislike doing before giving them a task.

30. Help New Volunteers Get Off On the Right Foot

Most great volunteers are made, not born. They require some training and education about your organization, but, most of all, they need encouragement and confidence boosting.

Put yourself in a newcomer's shoes: They have been asked to do an important job that is new to them, and they aren't being paid. They want to make a good impression and need occasional affirmation that they are on the right track. They may have had a previous unpleasant volunteer experience with another organization and were ready to give up volunteer endeavors for more lucrative pursuits or rewarding hobbies.

The way you work with a new volunteer may improve his or her perception of helping others. As a volunteer manager, your words of praise will carry considerable weight. With this in mind, here are some pointers to boost volunteers' confidence:

> It's important to be clear about your expectations of new volunteers. Eliminating any possible confusion makes the task at hand more meaningful for everyone involved.

✓ **Be clear about your expectations.** Don't be too reluctant to ask new recruits to do a crucial task, if you know they are well-suited to the job. But do offer a specific outline of deadlines and a list of persons to contact for assistance, then invite them to call you directly if obstacles are encountered that may impede their efforts.

✓ **"I know you can do it"** is a powerful remark and show of confidence. When possible, make favorable comments about their previous successes in the workplace or community. "We are so lucky to have you on board," will keep them inspired to not let you down.

✓ **Be unfailingly sincere in your praise.** Don't invent a compliment just for the sake of saying something nice. Keep your eyes open for an act genuinely worthy of praise, then seek out the individual to explain why you were impressed by his/her competence, kindness or diplomacy.

✓ **Express your confidence publicly.** Each time you meet with your committee or group, note the newcomers and make positive remarks about them. Your show of confidence will encourage others to join in with praise for the newcomer.

✓ **Thank them with a brief note or small gift.** The smallest token of appreciation, even putting a whimsical gold star sticker on their lapel at a meeting, will be a heartwarming gesture.

✓ **Be creative.** Make a short list of fun inexpensive ways to say thanks. Ask your board chair to send a personal note of appreciation. Produce a news release that speaks of your organization's anticipated accomplishments with the addition of new volunteers, and list their names.

Your attention to confidence-building will not only motivate new volunteers to assume a more active role, but will also help you cultivate those who will one day rise to positions of leadership within your organization.

31. Set Quantifiable Objectives For Volunteers

Avoid being vague about expectations. Instead, provide new volunteers with quantifiable goals that will give them something to shoot for.

Whether you're planning a single project that involves volunteers or developing a comprehensive operational plan for the upcoming year, it's in everyone's best interest to establish quantifiable objectives for volunteers.

In fact, work with the volunteers involved to draft those objectives together. If volunteers are a part of developing the objectives, they are more likely to own them and follow through with them.

Here are a few examples of quantifiable objectives developed for either individual volunteers or a group of volunteers:

- Recruit five new volunteers/members during the course of the year.
- Attend a minimum of 10 out of 12 regularly scheduled meetings during the year.
- Contribute a minimum of two hours each month throughout the fiscal year.
- Sell a minimum of 20 tickets per volunteer for an annual fundraiser.
- Identify at least three cost-saving ideas for the agency during the course of the year.
- Volunteer for at least one project without having to be asked to do so.

Examine what it is you most want your volunteers to accomplish, then break it down into achievable and quantifiable parts. They will be more likely to succeed if expectations are clear.

32. Dos and Don'ts for Defining Volunteer Roles

Be realistic in describing expectations of new volunteers' tasks, time commitments and deadlines.

Creating a volunteer job description is the first step for assigning the correct person to any volunteer role. Recruiting volunteers under a general umbrella of volunteer can lump too many individuals with varied backgrounds and skills into the same generic category.

Gather your volunteer management staff and ask the questions, "What do we want this volunteer to do?" and "Where is our greatest need?" These questions will take you a long way toward defining volunteer roles within your nonprofit.

Follow this list of dos and don'ts when assigning volunteer job descriptions:

- ❑ Do set aside time for your management team to define volunteer objectives and specific roles.

- ❑ Don't take the task of setting volunteer roles lightly. Volunteers bring a wealth of skills and services to your organization, so it's important to treat this task as critical to your nonprofit.

- ❑ Do create a list of volunteer roles including a task sheet that details specific expectations about the role for the volunteer.

- ❑ Don't create a list of impossible expectations. Be realistic about the time allotted for each volunteer role and ensure that the expectations of the role fit the time frame. Creating an extensive list for a 10-hour-per-month volunteer role will only ensure a feeling of failure by the volunteer.

- ❑ Do list the skills the volunteer will need to successfully fulfill the role. Are computer skills, people skills or technological skills needed? If so, be sure to include as much detail about the required skill set as possible to avoid assigning the wrong volunteer to the role.

- ❑ Don't ask the volunteers to take on the slush pile of work that staff refuse to do. Expecting a volunteer to take on the least appealing work is a recipe for disaster.

- ❑ Do review the volunteer job descriptions to ensure that what has been determined among your volunteer management staff is reflected in the job descriptions. Also, ask current volunteers to review the volunteer job descriptions and offer their feedback.

33. Boost Recruitment by Publicizing Your Philosophy

FUSION, a Federal Way, WA-based nonprofit providing housing and support services to the homeless, is an all-volunteer organization. Needing a constant stream of new supporters to maintain mission-related work, officials use a formal volunteer philosophy to assist volunteer recruitment efforts.

What goes into a volunteer philosophy? "Our mission statement has always been central to everything we do, and the volunteer philosophy is really an outgrowth of that," says Peggy LaPorte, founder. "Volunteers are the heart of our mission."

A philosophy statement sets expectations and helps prospective volunteers understand on what principles an organization was founded, says LaPorte. "It sets a tone for what an organization is all about, and explains how it and its volunteers will go about achieving their goals."

A volunteer philosophy is best developed by a board of directors, ideally with the input of an advisory council of community leaders and businesspeople, says LaPorte. She also says ensuring volunteers are treated with respect should be a top priority. "It's one of the most important ingredients in keeping an organization able to grow and sustain itself," she says. "If volunteers don't feel appreciated, they will walk away in an instant."

If you're interested in elements a volunteer philosophy might include, take a look at FUSION's published philosophy, shown at right.

Source: Peggy LaPorte, Founder, FUSION, Federal Way, WA. E-mail: laportepeggy@ yahoo.com

Your volunteer philosophy will help to attract individuals who are most compatible with your organization's programs and services.

Content not available in this edition

34. Covering the Mentor Gap

Consider having mentors assist your new volunteers in different capacities.

Sometimes a small tweak can make all the difference in a new program's success. While the mentoring program at the Atlanta Humane Society (Atlanta, GA) has proven very successful, one of the main challenges staff have faced is having enough mentors to keep up with the number of new volunteers. Director of Community Relations Tracy Lopez says that problem was exacerbated early on by offering two separate mentor sessions — one for cats and one for dogs.

"If volunteers were interested in working with both cats and dogs, they would have to attend two 2.5 hour sessions, and much of the same information was repeated," says Lopez. "We were also struggling with having enough mentors to meet the demand for mentor shifts. We've since changed the mentoring program to now consist of one large session broken into separate stations so that volunteers are mentored in both cats and dogs, in addition to administration. We now need fewer mentors and are able to accommodate as many as 10 volunteers per session!"

Source: Tracy Lopez, Director of Community Relations, Atlanta Humane Society, Atlanta, GA. E-mail: volunteer@atlantahumane.org

35. Make Your Volunteers Feel Special

Never stop evaluating the ways in which you make new volunteers feel welcome and special.

Don't take your important volunteers for granted. Let them know — often and in myriad ways — how special they are. Here are some ideas for doing so:

- Call them by name when you see them.
- Stop by to say hello as they work.
- Select a volunteer of the week, month and year.
- Provide volunteers with a suggestion box — and listen to what they suggest.
- Give them a discount on merchandise.
- Provide them with a free meal or gourmet coffee drink.
- When a celebrity or someone of note visits, bring him/her to meet your volunteers.
- Devote a bulletin board or other space to volunteer news.
- Get a business to sponsor the cost of several volunteer recognition perks — meals out, movie tickets, theater tickets and more.

36. Help Volunteers Realize Challenging, Achievable Goals

It's not enough to simply set goals for new volunteers. They need to know you're ready and willing to support them in achieving those goals.

As you know, people are motivated for different reasons. Nevertheless, most individuals are gratified when they make achievements. That's why it makes sense to look at each of your volunteer programs to determine what can be done to make it more goal oriented.

As you examine each program, keep these achievement principles in mind:

- ❑ Include intermediate as well as overall goals.
- ❑ Include appropriate incentives and/or celebrations with corresponding achievements.
- ❑ Identify a variety of achievement goal types — those for individuals as well as groups. This gives everyone an opportunity to accomplish something.
- ❑ Allow volunteers input in determining challenging yet achievable goals.
- ❑ Once goals have been set, monitor progress through regular meetings, updates in correspondence and other ways.

People enjoy winning causes, so do what you can to help them win along the way.

37. Recognize How Children Can Motivate Adult Volunteers

What drives your volunteers? Your ability to discern what motivates each of your volunteers will help bring them to new levels of accomplishment.

Children are an often-overlooked motivator for many adults. It's amazing how some people will rise to the occasion when little ones are involved — as recipients of the good deeds, as young observers or as volunteer participants.

Involve children in any of the following ways, then measure the difference doing so makes among the adults:

- Have children thank volunteers face-to-face or with handwritten notes.

- Put a young person in charge of a project you know he/she is capable of carrying out. It will be difficult for adults to say no to him/her when asked to help.

- Have a youngster read and distribute volunteer awards. It will make the volunteers receiving the awards melt.

- As appropriate for your organization's mission and specific volunteer duties, invite volunteers to bring their children or grandchildren along to assist them in their volunteer tasks or as guests at your volunteer banquet or recognition ceremony.

Consider the role young ones can play in motivating new volunteers and keeping them enthused.

38. Create No-frills Training, Opportunities for Busy Volunteers

In today's on-the-go society, time is tight for many people. Their jobs demand most of their attention; they're working and raising families; they're multitasking throughout their day; often, they have very driven personalities.

Yet, many such people may be willing to volunteer when they are able to do so on their own time and terms.

How can you accommodate these individuals who want to make a meaningful contribution and then get on with their lives? How can you convince them that you will meet them on their terms? Try these proven methods:

- Develop a menu of specific tasks from which they can choose that include brief job descriptions and the time estimated to complete each duty.

- Avoid offering volunteer jobs in which outside factors — setting appointments with others, tasks that involve waiting — may impede the timely completion of their responsibilities.

- Eliminate any frills — socializing, waiting for others to arrive, etc. — that prevent these volunteers from starting and finishing projects on their time.

- Keep training time to the point and as brief as possible. Consider sending training material in advance to avoid using on-the-job time for that purpose.

- Provide them with multiple choices of times to show up and complete tasks.

Help for New Volunteers

Match veterans with rookies. If others have experience with the task at hand, pair them with unexperienced volunteers. Doing so helps ensure that projects will be completed as well as in the past, and new volunteers will be prepared to take over when seasoned ones decide to move on.

- Err on the side of protecting their time. If, for instance, a task has not yet been fully completed by the time the volunteer said he/she would need to leave, have another volunteer prepared to step in and complete it for him/her.

Chances are good that you can keep these no-frills volunteers coming back, if you can accommodate their demands early on in your relationship with them. Although each volunteer commitment may be a brief in-and-out experience — or even involve their working from home — they will come to claim your organization as their own in time.

39. Correct Assignment Helps Start New Volunteer Off Right

A great match of talent and job assignment can make for a great volunteer.

When interviewing new or prospective volunteers to determine appropriate assignments, ask questions such as these to best match their skills with organizational needs:

✓ With what age groups are you most comfortable?

✓ If you had to choose between doing research in a quiet room or serving as a greeter at a public function, which would you prefer and why?

✓ Which do you prefer — asking someone for something or being asked for something?

✓ Imagine having volunteered with our agency for one year. What would you have accomplished during that time and why?

Give Volunteers a Pat on the Back

Want a visible way to praise volunteers? Try enlisting the help of staff by providing them with colorful paper/plastic buttons boldly printed with the word "PAT." The buttons should have peel-off double-sided tape on the back.

Staff can thank volunteers with a pat on the back, by attaching a button to the back of their shirt. As volunteers amass a collection of pats on the back, their sense of pride will grow along with the conversation value of this visible sentiment.

---

40. Extend A Welcoming Hand at Your Organization's Door

How does your organization welcome a new volunteer? Common ways of doing so include sharing your own experience, partnering them with an experienced volunteer or staff member, or offering them a tour.

Before any of that happens, why not begin by simply meeting them at the door?

Whether it's yourself, a direct supervisor or one of your constituents, a warm smile and greeting will go a long way in making a newcomer feel welcome.

This may sound like a small gesture, but it can be very comforting to someone new within your organization.

41. Celebrate Volunteer Birthdays

At the Mississippi Valley Regional Blood Center (MVRBC) of Davenport, IA, each of the 400 volunteers receives a special honor once a year in the form of a birthday card.

"This is a simple gesture from the company to say 'Happy birthday, and have a great day," says Kay Parch, manager of volunteer relations. Cards are signed "MVRBC" so recipients know they come from the entire blood center staff.

Granted, some individuals are more reserved that others, but who doesn't like being noticed on their birthday?

To honor your volunteers, Parch says:

✓ Consider purchasing discounted cards in bulk. Parch buys cards from It Takes Two, a Minnesota-based company that specializes in wholesale greeting cards for volunteers, at a cost of $1 a card.

✓ Create a fund or budget item that will fund the cards and postage. If budget is a concern, consider hand-delivering cards to volunteers during their volunteer shifts on or around their birthdays.

✓ Consider sending e-mail greetings from services such as Blue Mountain Greeting where, for a minimal membership fee, cards can be sent via e-mail. Most such companies offer free trial periods.

✓ Find a greeting card supplier or online service that lets you plug dates into an online calendar and sends you e-mail reminders of the impending day.

Source: Kay Parch, Manager of Volunteer Relations, Mississippi Valley Regional Blood Center, Davenport, IA. E-mail: kparch@mvrbc.com

42. Stay Tuned In to Identify Volunteers' Life Cycles

One of the primary reasons volunteers agree to assist an organization is because they enjoy contributing their skills and knowledge for a worthwhile cause. But they also have a variety of reasons for choosing your particular institution, such as working with their friends, having more opportunities to be assigned to jobs they love to do, and identifying strongly with your mission and purpose.

When the combination of these reasons are well balanced, volunteers may spend many years generously offering time and talents to your cause. But if these reasons change and they no longer feel a solid bond with the organization, their enthusiasm will likely weaken as well.

Because both your organization and individual volunteers are constantly active and evolving, changing or expanding in scope, a natural cycle of involvement typically exists between most organizations and their volunteers. And even if the volunteer naturally becomes less active, he/she will be able to pass the baton to a newer volunteer waiting for a chance to do the same job with a different approach.

Realizing that the natural life cycle of volunteering varies greatly from person to person, consider these approaches to keeping the flow moving in an orderly direction, to help ensure more seamless transitions as changes inevitably occur within the structure of your volunteer team:

- **Determine the length of service for key positions.** When you have an unusually talented group of volunteers together, ask if they would commit to a term of two to three years and train a replacement group during their last year. Your new group will have a strong background for their duties, and have time to see others in action who may be qualified to replace them. When lengths of service are predetermined, no one will be offended when it is time for them to take on a different assignment, and may enjoy their duties more fully knowing that it won't be a lifetime commitment.

- **Communicate with volunteers who are especially valuable.** All volunteers are appreciated and highly valued, yet some stand out as gifted and innovative. They may have more than one skill to share, but still have difficulty finding a niche within your organization. Work as closely with them as possible, even offering a five-year plan with the combination of variety and consistency they seek as a volunteer.

- **Establish both long- and short-term responsibilities.** Some volunteer duties, such as chairmanships of major events, fall neatly into a one-time category. A past chairman can then become an advisory chairman or honorary chairman. But other assignments benefit from consistency and prior experience. Ask volunteers how they feel about doing the same job more than one year — they may be eager to serve a second time after having learned the ropes, or they will know the job is not right for them. Making the effort to accommodate either preference benefits both you and your volunteers, keeping them satisfied longer.

- **Find a place for both one-time and lifetime volunteers.** Depending on their individual personalities and skills, some volunteers will be straightforward about how long they intend to be involved with your organization. They may have career or family plans that affect their length of service, hope to make contacts in as many organizations as possible, or want to offer the same skill to more organizations rather than doing many jobs for just one. Graciously accept volunteer help on the volunteer's terms. One person offering expert assistance on a one-time basis when it is most needed can be as beneficial as years of service by a marginally enthusiastic lifetime member. Both types are valuable, but for different reasons.

When it has become clear that one of your volunteers has lost enthusiasm for your causes, no one is benefiting and efforts may even be impeded, so it may be time to let them go. Even though volunteer managers are sorry to see this happen, it may be only a natural part of that particular volunteer's natural life cycle with your organization. However, those individuals may be willing to continue to serve as an occasional advisor — asking them to consider this will leave the door open for them to return, if they have a change of heart.

Be careful not to bore new volunteers with the same task over and over again. Be ready to shake it up if that will help to keep them energized.

43. Nurture Achievement to Motivate Volunteers

Identify what it is that most motivates each of your volunteers, then turn to methods that address that key motivator.

Who among your existing volunteers are energized by making achievements? By identifying those individuals, you can motivate them by:

✓ Offering feedback.

✓ Incorporating competition.

✓ Providing responsibility.

✓ Furnishing goals.

✓ Sharing problems that they will perceive as challenges.

✓ Providing quantifiable parameters allowing them to measure their success.

✓ Sharing past achievements that existing volunteers can work to surpass.

44. Assign Coaches, Assistants for Better Volunteer Oversight

If your nonprofit services include course instruction, consider assigning skilled volunteers as coaches and assistants.

The Computer Training Bridge (Winston-Salem, NC) provides free computer literacy classes for the Forsyth County community in North Carolina, reaching nearly 350 people a month with 73 skilled volunteers.

To manage its services most effectively, staff with the library's Computer Training Bridge program assign volunteers to computer coach and assistant roles. Ali Shoaf, project coordinator, tells us how these supervisory volunteer positions aid the organization:

❏ **Computer Coaches:** The computer coach is responsible for teaching course material to a class. Classes may range from four to 18 participants depending upon the size of the computer lab. They are responsible for picking up handouts and printing the rosters for their class using our online scheduler. Computer coaches offer their own passion for technology as well as their individual teaching styles. They are matched with course content based on their interest and comfort level and with a computer lab location based on close proximity to their work or home.

❏ **Assistants:** Assistants are volunteers scheduled for larger classes or classes where extra attention is needed. Assistants are responsible for setting up and closing the lab (turning on and off computers, logging in and out, setting up projectors and more) and helping class participants who may be struggling to follow the coach at times. All volunteers receive an orientation to the program and then serve as an assistant in classes until they are asked to lead a class as a computer coach.

"Our skilled volunteers help us increase digital literacy rates by allowing the program to extend the number of classes taught, extend the breadth of the program to offer classes in a variety of neighborhood computer lab settings and expand the range of classes offered to include specialties from each instructor," says Shoaf. "For example, we have fiscal analysts teaching (Microsoft) Excel, a Web developer leading Web design, an accountant leading QuickBooks and a retired minister teaching beginner classes to seniors."

Source: Ali Shoaf, Project Coordinator, Forsyth County Public Library in partnership with WinstonNet, Computer Training Bridge Program, Winston-Salem, NC.
E-mail: shoafa2@forsythlibrary.org

Specialized Recruitment Draws Volunteers With Special Skills

How does the Computer Training Bridge (Winston-Salem, NC) secure volunteers with specialized talents for the computer training program?

"We advertise online through a free volunteer resource in our community: www.handsonnwnc.org," says Ali Shoaf, project coordinator. "This resource is localized for our area but taps into a national database through partnering with 1-800-volunteer.org. Sixty percent of our volunteers come through this portal."

In addition, Shoaf says, they advertise the volunteer positions through Employment Security Commission of North Carolina (Raleigh, NC) and at the Forsyth County Public Library.

86 Ways to Build Long-term Relationships With New Recruits

45. Help Staff Accept and Support Your Volunteers

There are plenty of reasons why employees at your organization may have difficulty accepting and supporting volunteers: fear of job replacement; loss of control; lack of clarity between staff and volunteer responsibilities; and more.

To help your paid employees learn to be more accepting and supportive of volunteers, follow these steps:

1. Make employees aware of how volunteers are making a positive difference. Explain volunteer responsibilities and summarize achievements that have been made thanks to volunteer assistance.

2. Share the history of volunteer involvement at your organization. When did it begin and why? How has it evolved?

3. Show the human side of your volunteers. Share examples of volunteers' backgrounds and interests with employees.

4. Give examples of staff who have benefited from volunteer assistance. Better yet, have those employees share this information.

5. Get top management to convey their high level of support for volunteer involvement.

6. Share a procedure employees can follow if they might want volunteer assistance in their departments.

Show your employees the human side of your volunteers. Do your part to connect them with one another in multiple ways.

46. Online Management System Makes All the Difference

Lisa Munson, volunteer coordinator at Children's Hospitals and Clinics of Minnesota (St. Paul, MN), has been managing volunteer programs for years. She says using a Web-based volunteer portal has dramatically improved the way she does her job, and made her volunteers more productive.

"It's a two-prong system," says Munson. "It lets the volunteers track their own hours, and it lets us track the volunteers." The portal's calendar allows Munson to post events and requests, and lets volunteers easily see what's going on and where the needs are. They can respond to specific opportunities in which they're interested and sign up.

Munson says 10 years ago she tracked volunteer hours on paper. It was time-consuming, and only allowed her to gather total hours worked, not assess how and where volunteer hours were being allocated. Now she can run reports to see where her volunteers are working, where increases (or decreases) are occurring and much more.

They even use data discovered through running reports on the system to help them write their annual reports.

The most important thing, according to Munson, is that it's Web-based. "I can quickly check it at 9:00 on a Sunday night, and figure out what's going on the next day. We can also link it to our website, which is really nice."

For a volunteer manager, a quality online volunteer portal is like a compass, says Munson. "It's made me more productive, because I'm able to keep track of much more information than I could before. It helps us manage our volunteer resources, because it allows us to see exactly where our resources are being deployed."

One example involved their animal assisted therapy program. They noticed that requests for the service were increasing dramatically, and they were able to quickly re-allocate resources so they were aligned with the demand for services.

Their online volunteer portal was created by Volgistics. Munson says they pay an annual fee for the service.

A web-based volunteer portal serves as another way to communicate with and engage new volunteers.

Source: Lisa Munson, Volunteer Coordinator, Children's Hospitals and Clinics of Minnesota, St. Paul, MN. E-mail: volunteerservices@childrensmn.org

47. Familiarize Yourself With Volunteers' Non-volunteer Lives

Work at understanding what matters most to your new volunteers. What do they enjoy doing in their spare time? What drives them to want to volunteer? What fulfills them?

What do you know about the lives of your volunteers outside of their volunteer time?

By getting to know more about their personal and professional lives, you will do a better job of matching their skills and personal preferences with work opportunities. In addition, your enhanced insight will help to better nurture and support each volunteer based on his/her individual circumstances. To learn more about your volunteers:

- Meet one-on-one periodically to discuss both business and nonbusiness topics.
- When you come in contact with volunteers at work, take a minute to ask what is going on in their personal/professional lives.
- Maintain an open-door policy during designated times of the day or week.

48. Reduce Compassion Fatigue While Strengthening Resilience

If your organization's mission puts your volunteers, your staff and even yourself into highly stressful situations, be on the lookout for signs of compassion fatigue.

Compassion fatigue is the extreme state experienced by those helping others in distress and preoccupation with the suffering of those they are helping to the point of traumatizing the volunteer or helper. It can be a common ailment among volunteers who work with clients dealing with traumatic events, health issues or animal welfare.

Identify the red flags that can bring about compassion fatigue.

Kim Heinrichs, executive director of volunteer resources at San Diego Hospice and The Institute for Palliative Medicine (San Diego, CA), shares signs her organization uses to determine if someone is experiencing compassion fatigue:

- Inability to define healthy boundaries.
- Desire or need to fix patients' problems.
- Hesitation to share volunteer intervention with staff team members.
- Believing that patient can't survive without his/her help.
- Feeling of hopelessness as though nothing he/she does will make anything better.

Heinrichs shares steps to go from compassion fatigue to professional resilience:

- Take a break between patient or client assignments.
- Participate in supportive supervision meetings and volunteer continuing education and accept support from volunteer staff or coordinator.
- Discover and commit to personal self-care, including exercise, gardening, meditation and other forms of relaxation.
- Open communication between volunteer and staff to tackle potential patient or family challenges before they become a problem.

"Managers must understand that burnout is real and exists for both volunteers and staff," Heinrichs says. "Commit to best training and support practices by using training modules, available from national organizations such as the National Hospice and Palliative Care Organization (Alexandria, VA) and Volunteering in America (Washington, D.C.)." She recommends training modules that incorporate key topics such as saying goodbye, compassionate listening, boundary issues and best practices to educate and support volunteers.

Finally, Heinrichs says, be approachable and understanding, so volunteers will seek help from the management team. Enforce clear, ongoing communication between volunteer coordinators by instituting check-in calls to facilitate safe, open dialogue.

Source: Kim Heinrichs, Executive Director of Volunteer Resources, San Diego Hospice and The Institute for Palliative Medicine, San Diego, CA. E-mail: KHeinrichs@SDHospice.org

86 Ways to Build Long-term Relationships With New Recruits

49. Checklist Helps in Crafting a New Volunteer Position

Have you come to the conclusion that your organization could justify creating a new volunteer position?

If so, do your homework before asking your supervisors to approve the new position or recruiting volunteers to fill it.

Follow a planning checklist that ensures the new position has been well thought through, to reassure your superiors of its need and value, and to enable new recruits to hit the ground running when they assume their duties.

A checklist such as the one shown here will help you justify the position and plan for its effective implementation.

New Position Checklist

- ☐ Job description
- ☐ Qualifications of position
- ☐ Amount of staff support required
- ☐ Training required
- ☐ Anticipated budget needs
- ☐ Method of recruitment
- ☐ Areas of sensitivity/confidentiality
- ☐ Set hours/days per week
- ☐ Project timeline
- ☐ Work is done on- or off-site
- ☐ Adequate workspace and conditions
- ☐ Description of goals and objectives for the position
- ☐ Relationship of position to other volunteer and staff positions
- ☐ Methods for monitoring/supervising the position
- ☐ Methods for evaluating the position and completed work

50. Participate in Routine Duties to Inspire Volunteers

Envelope-stuffing is the quintessential example of uninspired manual labor that an organization's volunteers least like to perform. But letters have to be sent, and volunteers are often the most logical personnel to make it happen.

So what's an organization to do?

Try joining them. Having an executive director, volunteer manager or other senior staff member take part in mundane duties, even if only for 15 minutes, sends a powerful message that no job is unimportant or unnecessary when the mission is worthy.

If undertaken sincerely, occasional efforts like this provide volunteers with a long-lasting sense of meaning about otherwise thankless tasks. The conversation that arises will also provide an unmatched opportunity to answer volunteer questions, strengthen relationships with leaders and reinforce commitment to the organization's vision and values.

Give the gesture double impact by having the person who is stepping up to assist volunteers come bearing gifts — warm muffins, hot coffee or an invitation to move the task to his/her sunlight-drenched executive board room.

Be Accessible After Hours

Any phone call by a volunteer (or potential volunteer) to a closed office is almost a warning to the caller: "Call me at my convenience, not yours."

During evenings and weekends have an answering machine turned on to direct those who may wish to assist your efforts or need help with an assigned project. Including your home or cell phone number and even an e-mail address shows you are accessible even when the office is closed.

51. Looking for a New Team-building Activity? Try a Song

Many volunteer-based organizations use team-building activities to build camaraderie, nurture connections and provide a fun way for volunteers to bond. Some such activities harness the creativity and collaboration inherent in music.

What are you doing to build a sense of team spirit among your volunteers, both new and seasoned?

"Music is a universal interest, something anybody can contribute to," says Wallace Dunbar, director of development at Vanderbilt University's Owen Graduate School of Management (Nashville, TN). In 2010, Dunbar scheduled a song-based activity for the school's alumni, students and faculty through Kidbilly Music (Nashville, TN). "Some of the attendees were a little nervous about their singing ability," he says, "but it turned out to be a great way to break down barriers and help people get to know each other."

Kidbilly Music President Billy Kirsch says sessions are about telling an organization's story. "Every association, corporation and group has a story to tell. Writing a theme song together is a great way to help people articulate the things that make their organization great."

The team building begins with a session to brainstorm ideas about what the organization does, what its challenges are and what makes it unique, says Kirsch. Specially trained musical facilitators then help the group shape those ideas into lyrics and put them to music.

At the end of the two- to three-hour session, the group performs the song with guitar or piano accompaniment. A digital recording provides a takeaway to post on websites and blogs, publish on YouTube, and distribute internally as a morale booster, says Kirsch.

Dunbar says his organization posted the group's song on its website and featured it at an annual donor recognition dinner. "The song highlights what it means to be part of the Owens family," he says. "It's a great way to show the interesting and nontraditional kinds of activities our MBA program offers."

Though rates vary for different services, Kirsch says a half-day retreat typically costs $50 to $80 per person.

Sources: Wallace Dunbar, Director of Development, Owen Graduate School of Management, Vanderbilt University, Nashville, TN. E-mail: wallace.h.dunbar@ Vanderbilt.edu
Billy Kirsch, President, Kidbilly Music, LLC, Nashville, TN. E-mail: billy@kidbilly-music.com

---

One Group's Experience With Music-based Team Activity

Wondering if a musical team builder is right for your group? Erin Evans, director of client training at the Affinion Group (Stamford, CT) shares her organization's experience using Kidbilly Music (Nashville, TN), for a music-driven team builder:

What do participants get from this that they wouldn't get from, say, a ropes course?

"I think there is something equally inherently scary about having to be creative in a team building exercise — after all, you could fall flat on your face! I think that asking people to come together to build something creative forces us to work together in a way that we might not have tried before. Much like a ropes course, participants learn to trust each other by sharing insights and ideas — and in the end, our experience was that we found a lot of common ground."

Was your group excited about the activity, or somewhat reluctant?

"Somewhat reluctant. Most of the people who attended weren't very musical, but Billy (Kirsch, president of Kidbilly Music) and his team made it very easy to get started. He had an understanding of our business and provided some initial lines and melodies to get us thinking and sharing."

What were participants' reactions to the exercise when it was done?

"They were all enthusiastic about the end result. It was a lot of fun to get together with our other group and hear both songs being performed."

Have you used the recording of the song since the activity?

"Yes, we received CDs and shared the MP3s of the recordings with other departments internally. I listen to our songs probably once a month. It is a good reminder that we're all working to achieve the same goals."

Source: Erin Evans, Director of Client Training, Affinion Group, Stamford, CT. E-mail: Erin.Evans@affiniongroup.com

52. Return Cards Help Ensure Project Completion

To ensure volunteers complete assigned projects on time, provide project completion notices that they can return via mail or e-mail to confirm tasks have been completed.

Knowing the cards are to be filled out and sent to your office provides an additional element of motivation for the volunteer: "My job is not complete until I have confirmed it on my project completion notice." In addition, not receiving a notice on time provides you with a legitimate reason to push the volunteer to do his/her part.

PROJECT COMPLETION NOTICE: Travis Medical Center Auxiliary

Name: _____   Phone: _____

Project Assignment(s)	Deadline Date	Date Completed	Comments

53. Give Volunteers, Newcomers a Reason to Volunteer

With people busier than ever now, your job as a volunteer manager is to give them a clear, compelling reason to volunteer.

Every communication you send or post for current and potential volunteers should include at least three ways that volunteering benefits the volunteers. Consider these:

1. **Volunteering is good for your health.** It's a proven fact, volunteering is good for you, emotionally and physically. According to the Corporation for National & Community Service, volunteering has a positive effect on physical and mental health,; volunteering lowers the rate of depression among those 65 and older; and volunteering increases levels of self-worth.

2. **Volunteering will bond your family.** Volunteering can be done as a family, and the family that volunteers together, stays together.

3. **Volunteering offers many unexpected benefits.** List, in detail, the benefits volunteers receive at your organization. Do they get a free lunch the day they volunteer? Free health checks? Free admission to your annual gala? Gift shop discounts? The chance to learn new skills or share their knowledge with others? Tell them!

New Volunteer Procedures

■ When new volunteers join your work force, take time to introduce them to staff and others with whom they will be working: customers, other volunteers, board members, even your nonprofit's CEO.

54. Ask Your Volunteers for Input

Your volunteers will obviously keep doing what they're doing if they find fulfillment in it. That's why it's important to periodically ask for their input in various ways — one-on-one meetings, surveys, suggestion box, etc.

Answers to these open-end questions will provide you with valuable feedback.

- If you were in charge, how might you change this job?
- How can we show you we care?
- What's most gratifying about what you do here?
- What do you find most challenging about this job (or working here)?
- What would it take to make you feel successful in this job?
- Is there anyone you would like to be made aware of your achievements here?

Most importantly, if you take the time to ask for input, be sure to follow up and inform your volunteers of the ways in which you're following up.

Ordinary as it may sound, the traditional suggestion box is one of many ways to seek input from both new and veteran volunteers.

55. Boost Volunteer Performance

Looking to enhance the performance of your staff and volunteers? Getting out of your own head and looking at the organization from another point of view gives a fresh perspective and sets the stage for success.

Try to understand new volunteers' positions throw their eyes.

Begin adopting this mind-set by considering — and answering — questions that arise from workers' daily experiences, such as:

- What are the expected outcomes of this assignment/project/task/event?
- What is supposed to happen? When?
- Why is this initiative important? How does it relate to the organization's wider mission?
- What should I have accomplished when the task is complete?
- What action steps or activities are needed to accomplish targeted outcomes?
- What are my parameters, limits and boundaries?
- Has this been done before? What was the result?
- What are the available resources?
- Who are my points of contact? Who are my immediate supervisors?
- Who is responsible for what tasks?
- What date is the assignment due?
- How will my performance be measured?

56. Mentoring Program Provides Segue From Training to Service

If the only downside to a new program is that it fills quickly, and you have volunteers waiting to attend, you have a bona fide success on your hands. That is the case with the one-on-one, hands-on volunteer mentoring experience offered by the Atlanta Humane Society (Atlanta, GA). Director of Community Relations Tracy Lopez says, "Mentor shifts fill quickly, and we do not have as many mentors as we would like, so new volunteers may have to wait a few weeks to attend a mentor session and begin volunteering."

Even if mentoring does no more than to make new volunteers feel comfortable in their roles, it's worth doing.

> *"New volunteers love the program and enjoy having their very own mentor to address their questions/concerns about volunteering with the society."*

Here's how the program works. Seasoned volunteers, who have consistently been with the shelter over six months, mentor newly trained volunteers during a two-and-a-half hour session. New volunteers are provided with a schedule of mentor sessions at their initial training and sign up for a session that fits their schedules best. During mentor sessions, volunteers are provided with additional one-on-one training in the following areas: administration (volunteer software training), cat mentoring and dog mentoring.

The mentoring program was implemented to help volunteers feel more comfortable during their first shift and to provide a one-on-one experience with a seasoned volunteer who can address specific questions/concerns, and it seems to be working. Lopez says, "New volunteers love the program and enjoy having their very own mentor to address their questions/concerns about volunteering with the society."

Lopez is hoping the mentor program will boost retention, as well. "During the initial training a good deal of information is given, and a new volunteer's first shift can be very intimidating," says Lopez. "We're hoping that if they are more comfortable from the beginning, they will continue to volunteer with us, and we will be able to retain more volunteers."

Source: Tracy Lopez, Director of Community Relations, Atlanta Humane Society, Atlanta, GA. E-mail: volunteer@atlantahumane.org

57. Recognition Idea: Photo Wall to Highlight Volunteers

Does your staff realize the multitude of services rendered by volunteers? If not, here is a great way to make them aware.

Tag along with volunteers on routine assignments. Take a camera and snap candid photos as they perform service or participate in meetings.

Develop the photos larger than usual. Mount them in interesting groupings on a long piece of colored butcher paper. (Such paper is available at many school supply stores.)

Choose a theme such as The Many Faces of Service. Create a quaint border by printing volunteer names around the outer edges. Now display the oversized poster in a high-traffic area.

You will be surprised at how much attention a photo wall gets. It is also a great visible reminder of just how much volunteers contribute.

Special Ways to Say Thanks

■ Find out what your volunteers enjoy collecting. Oftentimes collectibles are inexpensive — matchbooks, golf balls, postcards, etc. By keeping a list of who collects what, you can be on the lookout for these items and use them to say thanks in a personal way.

58. Hospital Volunteers: Tips for Staffing Your Gift Shop

Are you doing all you can to keep your gift shop volunteers happy and motivated?

Patricia Sterner incorporates fun and prizes into her management of volunteers at the University of Iowa Hospital Clinics Wild Rose Gifts (Iowa City, IA).

"Our director has encouraged us to give lots of praise and also give treats or gift certificates for good customer service or other behavior," Sterner says. "We actually have a written definition of customer service, and when we hear our volunteers using specific language relating to it, we do want to encourage it more."

To keep volunteers motivated, Sterner says she is always looking for contests with prizes. She even uses this concept to improve gift shop management techniques. For example, when the volunteer manager found that a clipboard that is used to record merchandise requests was not being used as much as intended, she hosted a name-the-clipboard contest. She plans to award the contest winner with a prize, "then put a big sign on the clipboard with the name," which she hopes will help volunteers remember to use this tool.

Sterner says that while she provides new volunteers with a volunteer handbook, she believes they learn better from watching and imitating staff behavior. She says gift shop managers also meet with their volunteers two or more times a year to review training and address concerns. "And once a year we try to have a party, no training, just fun!"

For Sterner, scheduling her 30 gift shop volunteers is simple: "Our volunteers work a specific time each week, for example, Monday mornings 9:30 to 12:30. Then I only have to find subs when they are absent."

Beyond scheduling and reward matters, finding the right volunteers — and working with them and their schedule outside of the gift shop — can make a major impact on their satisfaction and, ultimately, how long they stay with your organization.

Linda Dias coordinates gift shop volunteers at Butler Hospital (Providence, RI). She says many retirees enjoy volunteering at the gift shop, because it fits well with their schedules. The Butler Hospital Gift Shop doesn't have a specific schedule for volunteers, Dias says. Rather, volunteers work when it works for them. "Some do four hours a week, others do full days, it all depends on the individual."

What are you doing to nurture new volunteers assigned to your gift shop?

Sources: Linda Dias, Human Resource and Volunteer Coordinator, Butler Hospital, Providence, RI. E-mail: ldias@butler.org
Patricia Sterner, UIHC Wild Rose Gifts, Iowa City, IA. E-mail: patricia-sterner@uiowa.edu

59. Short-term Steps Build Long-term Relationships

Volunteer managers often feel stuck between a rock and a hard place when it comes to volunteer recruitment. Mission-critical goals are invariably long-term but the public's interest in volunteering often seems decidedly temporary.

It's a challenging issue, to be sure, but not one that can't be overcome, says Susan J. Ellis, president of Energize, Inc., a Philadelphia, PA-based volunteerism consulting firm.

Ellis offers some suggestions on how to build long-term volunteer commitments within your nonprofit.

> *Be honest about what's involved in volunteering for your organization. And if necessary, break work down into bite-sized pieces.*

What kind of volunteering experience are people generally looking for now?

"Volunteers are all different, of course, but there is no question that people generally prefer short-term assignments. One reason is that we are all busy and time-deprived. But another big factor is that volunteering has a reputation for being a bottomless pit. People don't want to commit the rest of their life to an agency they are just getting to know."

Are people less committed to volunteering than they used to be?

"Part of what people perceive as lack of commitment is just changes in the way the world works today. People don't commit to jobs for 20 years anymore. Jobs don't commit to them. People move more frequently. These general trends in society impact volunteering as much as anything else. It doesn't say anything about volunteers' commitment."

What can nonprofits do to encourage long-term volunteering?

"The most effective approach is to ask for a limited initial commitment — maybe a year, maybe the duration of a limited project — and then reapproach people once they have had a good experience with your organization. You have to gain people's long-term loyalty one day at a time."

What mistakes or misconceptions do nonprofits have about long-term volunteers?

"Nonprofits should be looking for long-term relationships, not long-term commitments. Even if a person volunteers for only three weeks, you need to maintain that relationship, keep him or her willing to consider another project, and grow the system.

"Volunteer managers could learn a lot from fundraising people about cultivation. If you give $50 to a fundraising office, they create a file for you and start doing long-term cultivation work, so the organization will be in your will when you die. The whole idea of cultivation is much less understood in the volunteering world. Many nonprofits seem to have an attitude of, 'If you won't be here for twenty years, we don't want to bother with you,' which is very short-sighted."

What advice do you have on volunteer recruitment strategies?

"Use self-screening as a recruitment tool. If you have a narrow volunteering opportunity, you are much better served by writing a specific description that draws two people who are interested and qualified, than writing a general description that draws 80 responders, only two of whom actually want to do the work. It is better to let potential volunteers self-screen by appealing to the highest common denominator than to attract everyone, and have to take staff time to sort through them all."

Source: Susan J. Ellis, President, Energize, Inc., Philadelphia, PA. E-mail: Susan@energizeinc.com

---

Buck the Trend, Divide the Work

Susan Ellis, president of Energize, Inc. (Philadelphia, PA) offers two more suggestions for making the most of your volunteer relationships:

- Take pride in challenging the trend of quick and easy. If your volunteering opportunities are naturally long-term or commitment-heavy like Big Brothers/Big Sisters, make a point of emphasizing the hard work and stamina they will require (along with the lasting change that comes only from doing something hard), says Ellis. Appeal to people who like challenges.

- Structure work in bite-sized packages. Building long-term relationships is one half of a successful volunteering approach, but effectively involving short-term volunteers is the other. Ellis says restructuring work into self-contained tasks — ones with a clear beginning, middle and end — not only attracts new volunteers by offering them a low-commitment way to test the water, it can sometimes be the most effective way to get work done.

60. Give New Volunteers a Hand

To familiarize new recruits with your organization and those with whom they might come in contact:

1. **Provide directions to your facility or office.** Provide new recruits with printed directions to your facility or meeting place, including where, specifically, to report for their first shift.

2. **Host a casual reception for a new group of volunteers, along with staff at the end of the work day.** Give both staff and volunteers a chance to get acquainted right off the bat.

3. **Provide a complete tour of your facilities.** Volunteers will have a better understanding of how their jobs fit into the big picture, if they know what the big picture looks and feels like.

Consider having some sort of periodic welcoming reception or get-together for your new volunteers.

61. Daily Bread Takes Volunteer Descriptions to the Next Level

More than 10,000 volunteers are an essential part of Daily Bread Food Bank's (Toronto, Ontario, Canada) workforce. Using a detailed job description provides incoming volunteers a road map to success and a document that will help them determine if the position is aligned with their skills.

The current opening of Advocacy Support Worker is no exception to the detailed role descriptions (sample shown below) available at Daily Bread. This role description offers in-depth details of all aspects of the position, which enables the volunteer staff at Daily Bread to locate the best person for the position.

To provide transparency and identify the best individual for any given role, consider adding the following details to your volunteer role descriptions.

- **Hours:** Use the role description form to outline the hours required and the minimum commitment needed. Daily Bread's Advocacy Support Worker description details three to six hours per week and a three-month commitment.

- **Training:** Detail the required training needed to fulfill and succeed within the position, along with the number of hours and timing of the training involved. If training requires five evening sessions in a row, be sure to spell that out here to avoid unnecessary expenditure of time on the wrong candidate.

- **Position Purpose:** After providing a detailed overview of your organization and the volunteer role, drill down deeper by adding a specific section that details the position's purpose. Take time to outline how this role fits into the larger picture of your organization.

- **Duties:** Spell out specific duties for each position posted. Avoid glossing over any duties that will be required of the individual that may be deemed unappealing, as it's best to offer more details than not to find the right candidate for the role.

- **Skills/Qualifications:** Make sure to list any specialized needs or skills required for the volunteer role. Consider offering a training period which allows a volunteer candidate ample time to obtain the training needed, allowing more individuals to be eligible for the role.

Source: Alisha Coroa, Volunteer Coordinator, Daily Bread Food Bank, Toronto, Ontario, Canada. E-mail: Alisha@dailybread.ca

Content not available in this edition

62. Volunteer Turnoffs to Avoid

Be on the lookout for volunteer turnoffs and take steps to eliminate or at least diminish them.

As you assess volunteer programs and work to make them the best they can be, strive to eliminate these 14 volunteer turnoffs:

1. Lack of cooperation.
2. Unclear roles and objectives.
3. Misrepresented time expectations.
4. Lack of clarity regarding leadership.
5. Poor meetings with lack of focus.
6. Inadequate training and education.
7. Not being able to accomplish desired goals.
8. Having ideas be ignored.
9. Misrepresented goals and objectives.
10. Meaningless job assignments.
11. Being drawn into disputes.
12. Staff exhibiting lack of confidence.
13. Staff who intimidate.
14. High staff turnover.

63. Novel Orientation Trains, Screens Volunteers Simultaneously

The Wake Forest University Baptist Medical Center (Winston-Salem, NC) has over 600 volunteers attending orientations each year. The volunteers perform important, sensitive work, which requires an orientation that offers both a selection process and training. Volunteers attend an orientation before having an interview that ultimately determines whether they serve at the hospital. The orientation gives both the hospital and potential volunteer the opportunity to see if there is a good fit.

Eleven two-hour orientation sessions are held throughout the year. On average, 30 to 60 volunteers attend, but as many at 100 to 200 take part during the busiest months. These sessions are led entirely by staff and cover the following topics:

Sometimes an orientation process also serves as an additional way to screen new volunteers.

- History of the medical center
- Safety and security
- Customer and patient satisfaction
- Confidentiality and HIPPA
- How to utilize pastoral care
- Screening and the interview
- Paperwork required to apply for a volunteer position
- Abuse training — how to recognize and report abuse
- Expectations, time commitment, skills needed and available positions
- Next steps (e.g., when to expect a call for an interview)

The orientation acts as a natural screening process as volunteers learn expectations as well as required skills before committing to serve. On average 90 to 95 percent of attendees move on to the interview process. Each volunteer must also pass a criminal background check before starting. During the interview the hospital gets to know potential volunteers more intimately to determine suitability and where to best place them. Questions asked during the interview include:

- Why did you choose Wake Forest Baptist Medical center as a place to volunteer?
- What special skills will you bring?
- What are your interests and where would you like to serve?

Director of Volunteer Services Susan Washabaugh explains that having the orientation before volunteers are approved has improved efficiency. "In the past some volunteers would be approved and commit to serving. However, after being placed and starting training, something would come up where they could not attend the orientation. This was a liability for the medical center, so the volunteer had to stop volunteering until he/she could attend orientation the next month. Now volunteers are required to attend orientation prior to their interviews. We set the expectations up front, so volunteers know what they are required to do. It is a win-win process for both parties."

Source: Susan Washabaugh, Director of Volunteer Services, Wake Forest University Baptist Medical Center, Winston-Salem, NC. E-mail: swashaba@wakehealth.edu

Nurturing New Volunteers

86 Ways to Build Long-term Relationships With New Recruits

64. Set Aside Correspondence Time

There's nothing more personal and appreciated than a handwritten letter or note — especially in this day of e-mails, texts and tweets.

When someone goes out of his/her way to write and bring one up to date on important and not-so-important matters, or to say thank-you for a job well done, it is meaningful and appreciated.

Make a point to write personal notes and letters to volunteers regularly. Set aside one day each month to write birthday cards, notes recognizing their volunteering birthday, as well as just-because notes. Share insider information, let them know you're aware of what they are contributing, and leave them with a lasting memory of why their assistance means so much.

Relationship-building Tip

- It's been said that "when you start relationship building and then stop, it's worse than not having started at all." Know that each new introduction requires ongoing attention and nurturing.

---

65. Incentivizing Program Makes Service More Rewarding

Offering volunteer rewards can be a simple way to increase volunteer retention. At the Norfolk Public Library (NPL) of Norfolk, VA, volunteers are rewarded based on the number of hours served as follows:

- 25 hours = 1 NPL Book Sale item voucher
- 50 hours = NPL water bottle
- 100 hours = NPL CD holder
- 200 hours = movie tickets
- 300 hours = NPL lunchbox/cooler
- 400 hours = NPL nylon drawstring sport pack
- 500 hours = NPL logo shirt

In addition to earning gifts for hours served, Amanda Lloyd, volunteer and training coordinator, rewards the library's 175 volunteers with a gift during National Volunteer Week and during the holidays. This year, NPL volunteers received an umbrella adorned with the library's logo at the nonprofit's annual volunteer luncheon in April to mark National Volunteer Week. NPL's 2010 holiday gift was a candy-filled ceramic mug with the library's logo on it. The inexpensive gift cost the library approximately $3 per volunteer..

To fund the volunteer rewards program, the library has an active advocacy group called the Friends of the Norfolk Public Library who raise funds on behalf of library programs. Each year the group is able to raise an average of $3,500 for volunteer and training programs, the only funding Lloyd has all year.

"The rewards program gives volunteers something to look forward to based upon commitment. And we want to show our appreciation of them for that commitment with a small token of appreciation," says Lloyd. "It lets them know they're appreciated, and the volunteers love them! Our volunteers are often surprised and timid about receiving the awards."

Further Suggestions on Developing a Rewards Program

Are you interested in creating a rewards system for your volunteering program? Amanda Lloyd, volunteer and training coordinator at the Norfolk Public Library (Norfolk, VA) offers the following tips for developing a rewards program:

- Develop a group dedicated to annual funding, and solicit gifts donated by groups who believe in your mission. There are many organizations and businesses who donate money to important causes, determine where your nonprofit fits in and make the ask.
- Think about what kind of gifts you want to offer and work within your budget. Buy in bulk whenever possible to reduce costs.
- Figure the number of hours a week volunteers typically serve to determine the number of hours per incentive.

Source: Amanda Renwick Lloyd, Volunteer and Training Coordinator, Norfolk Public Library, Norfolk, VA. E-mail: Amanda.lloyd@norfolk.gov

2012 © Stevenson, Inc.

37

66. Seven Ways to Engage Power-motivated Volunteers

The desire to seek power is a natural motivator for some volunteers. When that's the case, use it to your advantage.

What strategies do you use to motivate volunteers? When seeking to encourage and lift up your valuable volunteer force, it helps to first know what drives a specific volunteer to give of his or her time.

Some individuals, for instance, are driven by power or the opportunity to be a part of something big, while others may be driven by a sense of achievement or an affiliation with others.

When seeking to motivate power-driven persons, keep these points in mind:

1. Choose assignments that allow them to rub shoulders with persons of authority and/or to personally gain increased responsibility and authority.

2. Provide them with opportunities that allow innovation.

3. Assign them tasks that allow them to teach or train others.

4. Publicize stories of their efforts in external and internal publications.

5. Find legitimate opportunities to seek their advice and suggestions.

6. Include them on your board.

7. Present them with awards and letters of commendation.

67. Achievement Begins With Staff

The only thing worse than having an enthusiastic volunteer coordinator with no volunteers is having an enthusiastic group of volunteers with an indifferent staff person who fails to provide guidance, support and motivation.

If you want to build an accomplished group of volunteers, it's important that you be there for them. Your role is crucial to their success. Follow each of these principles:

- **Show them what's expected.** Help your volunteers visualize both the outcome of their work and the steps required to complete their project. Provide a volunteer structure that gives organization to their efforts and helps provide them with the systems necessary to work on their own.

- **Support them.** Be available to answer questions or provide a meeting area. While you may expect your volunteers to accomplish work on your organization's behalf, you still need to guide the process and provide direction as necessary.

- **Keep them motivated.** See that their work remains meaningful. Don't allow them to get bogged down or diverted away from their primary objective. Recognize both individual and group accomplishments. Find inexpensive ways to reward their efforts.

You will find that those volunteer-driven projects with the greatest success have had a staff person in the background who provided the tools necessary to motivate and support the volunteers throughout the process.

Avoid Hassles With Written Volunteer Descriptions

Many nonprofits have formal descriptions for standing positions that are open to new volunteers year after year. But developing descriptions for more short-term positions such as special event workers can be a good idea as well. Defining such positions — including what duties volunteers are responsible for, whom they can go to when they have questions, what they should wear, what time they should report to their post and how to go on break when needed — can seem like a lot of work, and in some cases it is. But that work will repay itself many times over in reduced hassles, misunderstandings and problems on the day of your important event.

68. Empower Volunteers to Make Decisions

Free up your time and stop wasting energy on low-priority problem solving by empowering volunteers to make informed decisions. A wise manager will supply volunteers with ample knowledge and authority to handle ordinary problems.

Here are some suggestions:

Concentrate on Training
- Pack orientation sessions full of useful information.
- Answer the most frequently asked questions.
- Provide an orientation packet that reviews basic responsibilities, policies and procedures.
- Walk volunteers through solving problems common to your agency.

Provide Background
Often, knowledge of the history behind procedures/ policies is essential for making decisions on how to follow through. For example, a medical facility policy requires new mothers to be discharged from the hospital in a wheelchair, holding their infants in their arms. Liability and safety are the reasons for the policy. The history behind the policy involved an unmarried mother considering placing a baby for adoption. The father, present as the woman was discharged, insisted he carry the infant from the nursery to the car. At the hospital exit, he bolted across the parking lot, kidnapping the baby.

Armed with this additional insight, volunteers who discharge such patients will more likely enforce the policy or make an informed decision when the policy is challenged.

Furnish Resources
- Make necessary resources easily accessible to volunteers.
- When new situations arise, include solutions in resource materials.
- Provide contact names and phone numbers for physical facility concerns, security issues and emergencies.

Define Problem Resolution Hierarchy
Volunteers need to know where to turn when unable to solve a problem. They may report to a coordinator, who may report to a manager, who reports to the CEO. Generally, the problem can be resolved along the way. A volunteer should never go directly to the CEO.

Offer Reinforcement
When a volunteer makes a decision or independently resolves a problem, be sure he/she is complimented and recognized for accepting that responsibility. Confidence and mastery result from experience.

Knowledge is power. Armed with enough information, volunteers can relieve some of the stress on managers by accepting responsibility to resolve everyday problems within agency guidelines.

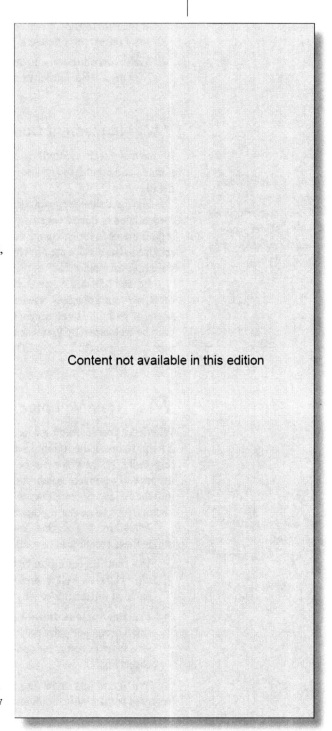

Content not available in this edition

69. Smart Volunteer Retention Tips

All nonprofits need a strong volunteer base to succeed and grow. To keep volunteers coming back for more:

- ✓ **Treat volunteers like clients.** Consider treating volunteers as though they are clients of your nonprofit. Nurture the relationship as you would a client's — offering ongoing support, care and attention. Create an environment of value, valuing volunteers who value your nonprofit.
- ✓ **Create an environment of show, not tell.** Post photo essays on your nonprofit's blog or website to show your volunteer board members, trustees and staff in action. Such posts reflect to volunteers how important their work is.
- ✓ **Make introductions.** Introduce volunteers to a client or recipient of your services. Nothing speaks louder than the gratitude of those persons you help.

70. Implement Condensed Volunteer Orientations

Often times it works to your advantage to condense or streamline the orientation procedure for new volnteers.

If your volunteer orientations span the course of a full day or more, consider offering more pointed and condensed trainings for volunteer roles that can operate with less need for detail.

Having volunteer positions filled by professionals from the community who are credentialed or have a specific educational background might allow you to streamline and reduce the need for extensive volunteer orientations. A volunteer with a specific degree relative to the service area in which they will work can get by with a bare bones approach to volunteer orientation.

Instead of using a one-size-fits-all approach to volunteer orientation, consider breaking your volunteer orientation into segmented areas that are more tailored to the needs of individual volunteers or specific groups. The variety of orientations will not only be welcomed by your incoming volunteers, but will also alleviate boredom of staff members conducting the trainings.

71. Train Volunteers by Breaking Jobs Into Parts

"Inch by inch, life's a cinch." — Break down what may appear to be overwhelming jobs into achievable components.

Whenever you're training a new volunteer to do a job that has multiple responsibilities, it helps to break the job into individual components. By focusing on each separate responsibility, the volunteer becomes more familiar with every aspect of that duty. For instance, if you were going over the job of volunteer receptionist, you might break training into the following components: phone etiquette, procedure for transferring calls, directing visitors, jobs to do during downtime, etc.

In addition to covering duties and issues associated with various volunteer positions, utilize these techniques to reinforce what's been said:

- **Use real-life examples to make your point.** Share past examples of projects that went right, as well as those that went wrong. Discuss how they could have been handled differently or why doing the right thing made a positive difference.

- **Practice various duties using mock situations.** Either assign participants to work in small groups or pairs practicing role-playing or invite two people from the audience — a veteran volunteer and a rookie — to act out a certain situation with everyone else observing.

You'll find that reviewing the various components of a volunteer's job will make him/her more comfortable, confident and able to perform effectively.

72. Take Steps to Recharge and Keep Your Outlook Positive

A big part of a volunteer manager's job is to keep volunteers and the staff who work with them upbeat, positive and focused on working together toward the greater good.

Most days, this cheerleader role may come naturally for you.

But what about days when it doesn't?

Do your part to stay positive and focused on your organization's mission while avoiding job burnout by giving yourself some breathing room now and then. Use these remedies to gain perspective and break away from routine:

1. Take one day out of each month to visit other volunteer-driven nonprofits. Discover what they're doing to recruit, retain and manage volunteers.

2. Designate at least one day during each quarter as chew-the-fat day. Take other staff and key volunteers to a pleasant environment to look at the big picture and talk about what's working and what's not working.

3. Spend some time each week walking your facility or campus, witnessing programs and services in action and reminding yourself how volunteers are making a noticeable difference in the lives of those you serve.

If you're enthused, your volunteers are much more likely to feel inspired as well. That's why it's important to "replenish" yourself regularly.

73. Keep Volunteers Updated With a News Book

For volunteer managers who do not have daily or weekly personal contact with all volunteers, getting messages out is difficult. A simple news book can solve the problem, especially if volunteers regularly check in at one or more central locations.

A news book may be a simple three-ring binder with an attractive cover, or it can take on the look of a newsletter. If volunteers report to more than one central location, make several identical books. It is important that all volunteers have easy access to the book(s), and that they make it a habit to review the book weekly.

1. **Divide the book into topics.** For example, you might post job openings, event announcements, sign-up sheets or policy changes.

2. **Use tabbed divider sheets, or colors, to separate topics.** Volunteers will want to quickly scan each section. To make it easy, print different topics on different brightly colored paper.

3. **Put time-sensitive information on top.** Insert the most important or time-sensitive information just behind the divider. This allows volunteers to quickly locate the current news.

4. **Update regularly.** Keep the book newsworthy by removing outdated materials and promptly posting fresh news. Remember, to update all books simultaneously.

5. **Initial mandatory reading.** Policy changes are high priority, for example. Provide space on a document, an additional page or a roster for volunteers to sign or initial as verification that they have read and understand mandatory information.

6. **Make it fun.** Besides hard business, the news book may contain a human interest or honorary section. Post thank-you notes, wedding/anniversary announcements or news clips. Recognize birthdays or volunteers of the month in this way.

Here's a communications tool that is useful with both new and experienced volunteers.

The news book may eventually replace a newsletter. A monthly letter from the volunteer manager or auxiliary president may be included.

As a secondary benefit, the news book, with its broad compilation of training materials, is beneficial to new volunteers. They can quickly gain insight into policies, procedures and corporate culture.

If the book is handled by many hands, consider placing sheets in plastic covers.

74. Nurture Creative Thinking

To get volunteers thinking creatively at your next planning meeting, try this:

Get attendees to think through the eyes of someone else. Ask them to write down the name of a famous person. Then put the challenge or issue facing your committee before them and ask them to solve the problem from the perspective of the individual each listed. Participants will have fun sharing their great opinions and may find a creative solution as well.

75. Test Ways to Make Routine Tasks More Fun

Bulk mailings, addressing envelopes, setting up and taking down displays after events are just some of the typically mundane jobs often assigned to volunteers. In fact, many volunteer jobs have routine but absolutely necessary chores attached to them.

But routine doesn't have to mean boring. Following are some tips for making routine chores more enjoyable and/or less time-consuming:

- **Offer a small incentive for quick work.** A little friendly competition can make jobs more fun for individuals or groups of volunteers. Rewards for speediest completion of tasks, such as a gift certificate, box of cookies or a gourmet loaf of bread, are examples of simple prizes you can offer.

- **Choose a pleasant location.** Invitation-addressing sessions or small meetings where routine business must be discussed will be more fun in a comfortable room, a lovely patio or someone's cozy kitchen. Offer a light lunch, tea, or a continental breakfast, depending on the time of day. Encourage casual working attire.

- **Hold a social gathering at a restaurant or coffee shop after the work is finished.** If volunteers enjoy meeting for a snack and conversation (as a reward for finishing the job), it can become a tradition after every business meeting or cleanup time.

- **Team people who enjoy each other's company.** Ask persons who get along well to work the same shift, and avoid pairing those who may have personality conflicts. At the same time, make an effort not to put slower volunteers together on the same task if time is an issue.

- **Combine tasks and festivities.** When possible, turn work into fun by choosing a festive theme for the activity. A potluck pickup party for cleaning up trash in a public park is an example. Let your creativity guide you to create fun themes.

- **Use many hands to make light work.** Consider trying to schedule routine tasks for a certain day of the week or month. Offer bonus volunteer hours or incentives for volunteers who show up to help on those predetermined days, or as a way to make up for missed shifts or assignments. Always have plenty of refreshments, supplies and sufficient work space available at these times.

- **Play pleasant background music or rent a good movie to watch during the task.** Many routine jobs require minimal concentration, so why not enjoy music or a newly released film that all would like to see?

- **Open any special attractions at your facility to your volunteers when they finish.** If your building has a swimming pool or fitness center, allow volunteers to use them on that particular day. They may volunteer more often, if they like your equipment or resources when a free workout is the reward.

Finally, simply ask your volunteers what they think is enjoyable, even offer a modest prize for the best idea to make work more fun. Make a list of all of the input received, then implement them into routine meetings for the rest of the year.

"Routine" need not equate into "boring." There are a variety of actions you can implement to make routine tasks for fun and energizing for new volunteers.

76. Positive Approaches to Retain Volunteers

Looking for ways to promote positivity within your nonprofit and spread cheer to volunteers?

Try these websites for insightful daily positive anecdotes to share with volunteers:

- Live Positivity
- Only Positive News
- Positive Quotes

77. Discover New Volunteers Fullest Potential by Conversing

The intake process for new volunteers can be time-consuming, but including a face-to-face conversation as part of that process can reap unknown benefits for your organization — particularly if your mission allows for many and varied volunteer roles and opportunities to fill.

For example, the Pittsburgh chapter of Dress for Success, which offers career-development services and professional attire to economically disadvantaged women, has many kinds of volunteer opportunities: sorting clothes, meeting with clients to choose attire, running client support groups, fundraising, special-event planning, helping out with administrative needs, etc. Even when a potential volunteer approaches the group with one kind of volunteer role in mind, it's helpful for both parties to have a conversation that might lead to other roles the volunteer is suited to fill.

Constance Mayer, director of programs and operations, explains, "In the initial meeting with the volunteer, I get a full profile of who the person is — where they work, what other groups they are involved in, what their passion is. An individual may contact us, and through our conversation I learn that she is active in a mom's group — a perfect candidate to run a maternity clothing drive. Or, she might work for a corporation that has matching funds for her time donated. When I realize what their skill set is, I offer as many ways to get involved as possible and see what they are willing and able to do, now and later."

Michael Aaron Glass, CEO of Dress for Success Pittsburgh, adds that it always pays to adopt an optimistic approach with every new volunteer. "Every clothing donor is not capable of being a financial donor, and every financial donor is not qualified to be an organization director. It is our responsibility to try to develop each contact to his/her fullest potential. (But) in a perfect world, we want to develop every contact. We would like to develop people who donate clothing into people who donate clothing and time, then money, and then, ultimately, to a full-time financial, time and talent donor up to, potentially, a member of the board of directors."

Volunteers having confidence in your organization is key, Mayer adds. "Most of our volunteers give of themselves as much as they possibly can, in whatever way they can. We find that our most committed volunteers really walk the talk in terms of time and money. This again goes back to the idea of having confidence in what your organization is doing, how it is spending its money and how well the staff is managing it."

Source: Michael Aaron Glass, CEO and Constance Mayer, Director, Programs and Operations, Dress for Success Pittsburgh, Pittsburgh, PA. E-mail: constance@dressforsuccesspittsburgh.org

Prioritize Direct Client Contact

No matter what kind of volunteer opportunities may be discussed with a potential volunteer, Constance Mayer, director of programs and operations at Dress for Success Pittsburgh (Pittsburgh, PA), always strives to include direct-client contact as part of the volunteer experience. It's the best way to ensure that each and every volunteer gets to "see the vision" of the organization, Mayer believes.

"When they volunteer to suit clients or speak to a group of unemployed women, the feeling they get from helping another woman cannot be communicated in any other way," Mayer says. "Direct client service is the most powerful experience for volunteers."

78. Confirm Volunteer Assignments in Writing

What tools do you provide your volunteers to help them succeed?

As you work with multiple numbers of volunteers on projects requiring their individualized follow-up, your odds of having them complete assigned tasks will improve significantly if you provide each volunteer with written confirmation of what it is he/she is supposed to do (and by when).

Whenever you conduct a meeting in which volunteers leave with agreed-to tasks, immediately send them a personalized memo — as opposed to a standardized group memo — confirming their duties. Spell out exactly what is expected of them, and be sure to include a deadline for the project (or multiple deadlines for portions of the project).

In addition to delineating each task, clearly state how to report back or turn in completed work. This helps bring closure to the task.

Here are two techniques you may want to include in your memo:

1. Offer an incentive for completing tasks on time.

2. Add a final sentence to your memo indicating that all persons not having completed their tasks by the stated deadline will be contacted by you (or the appropriate person) to determine what needs to happen in order to finish the project. Adding a closing statement such as this motivates volunteers to avoid the embarrassment of being contacted and provides you with a justifiable reason for following up with them.

Put new volunteers' assignments in writing so there's no question about what's expected and when it is to be completed.

January 3, 2012

St. Joseph's Hospital
FOUNDATION

TO: Tom Peterson, Sponsorship Committee
FROM: Brenda M. Hawley, Sponsorship Chairperson
RE: Calls to Be Completed By February 15
CC: Debra M. Brown, Director of Alumni

Thank you, Tom, for attending the December 13 Sponsorship Committee meeting and agreeing to call on the following businesses to serve as sponsors for our upcoming event.

As you know, it's imperative that we have commitments from these businesses by February 15 if we are to remain on schedule with our event timeline. For that reason, I am suggesting you schedule appointments for this week and next so business owners and managers have sufficient time to make a decision.

Please turn in (or fax) your completed calls to the Office of Alumni as you complete them. The fax number is 465-9097. As was mentioned at our meeting, those who turn in all calls on time will receive two 50 percent off coupons for dinner at Winchester's.

I encourage you to call me or Debra Brown if you have any questions, need any assistance or experience any difficulty that would impede your ability to complete these calls on schedule.

I will plan to contact any persons who have not turned in their calls to the Office of Alumni by February 15.

Thank you for your valuable assistance with this portion of our 2012 Celebrity Speaker Event.

Sponsorship Calls to be Completed by Tom Peterson by February 15:

- Benders Office Supply & Equipment
- Determan Pepsi Distributors
- Osborne Trucking, Inc.
- Klein Brokers
- Castrole Travel
- Peterson Photography
- MasterCuts
- Winston Raceway

Shown at left is an example of a memo confirming a volunteer's duties.

79. Five Effective Volunteer Appreciation Ideas

Without a doubt, volunteers are an invaluable resource to your nonprofit organization. Try these simple ways to show your valued volunteers exactly how much they mean to your organization:

✓ Frame a photo of the volunteer in action serving clients or helping your organization, along with a handwritten thank-you note mounted within the frame.

✓ Gather all volunteers and staff to join in an impromptu round of applause for a job well done by a specific volunteer or group of volunteers who have recently completed or are in the middle of a major project or difficult task.

✓ Create a giant banner of thanks to include the names of all volunteers and handwritten greetings from staff, clients and visitors.

✓ Ask a school class to adopt your nonprofit and create a poster about the service of volunteers to post for your volunteers to enjoy.

✓ Ask a community leader to take a special volunteer to lunch in appreciation of his or her selfless efforts for your cause.

What can you do for your volunteers that they will perceive as special? Here are a few ideas worth considering.

80. Intense Training Creates Committed Volunteers

Volunteers at the Trauma Intervention Program of Northern Nevada (TIP) in Reno, NV, complete 45 hours of training before embarking on their volunteer duties, which includes serving those who are emotionally traumatized in emergency situations. TIP volunteers are called to emergency scenes to assist family members, witnesses and bystanders. TIP is a national organization that offers emergency volunteer services in more than 250 cities.

Becoming a TIP volunteer requires a high level of commitment to complete a 45-hour training course over two weeks. Volunteers attending TIP training must complete all scheduled days of training without exception, and tardiness is strongly discouraged. Training includes classroom sessions, a ride with emergency personnel, a hospital tour and three months of field training. To ensure a high level of commitment, volunteers are asked to sign a one-year contract on the first night of training.

Another method to ensure volunteer recruits are serious about their commitment is a $50 registration fee and tuberculosis screening, both of which are paid by trainees. The registration fee helps cover the cost of bringing in two national trainers, as well as the cost of providing a training manual to each recruit.

According to Gabrielle Totton, Northern Nevada TIP director, it's not unusual to have about 25 recruits sign up for training and end with about 11 to 15 trained volunteers who are eligible to attend the graduation ceremony.

"Recruits often arrive on the first night unsure of what TIP is all about," says Totton. "As such, day one of training is dedicated to addressing what being a TIP volunteer means, what to expect from TIP and what we, as an organization, expect from each volunteer. That information is critical to recruits when determining if TIP is the right fit for them."

Due to the intensive nature of volunteer training, Totton finds it beneficial to offer a graduation ceremony upon completion of all training requirements. Graduating volunteers are honored at a ceremony complete with an audience of local dignitaries and invited guests. These volunteers receive a certificate of completion and official TIP badges engraved with their name, which replace their temporary trainee badges.

Source: Gabrielle Totton, Executive Director, Trauma Intervention Programs, Inc., Reno, NV. E-mail: Gabrielle@tipnnv.org

Take steps to help your new volunteers be committed volunteers.

86 Ways to Build Long-term Relationships With New Recruits

81. Five Ways to Connect with Achievement-motivated Persons

When working with volunteers who are motivated by a drive to achieve, be sure to:
1. Encourage their participation in goal-setting meetings.
2. Give them job assignments that offer increased responsibility.
3. Offer them recognition from top management acknowledging achievement.
4. Seek out quantifiable assignments that include benchmark points of success.
5. Offer them the opportunity to provide input and advice and challenge decisions.

82. Teach Volunteers Through Role-playing

To generate enthusiasm and boost the learning curve at your next volunteer in-service, incorporate role-playing into training workshops.

Here are some ideas to make your role-playing sessions more effective:
- ✓ Have participants act out situations that have actually happened in previous years as a way to learn how to handle the unexpected.
- ✓ Have trainees critique each other's role-playing and offer improvements. Be sure to stress the importance of pointing out what others are doing right as well as ways they can improve on their techniques or people skills.
- ✓ Look to your veteran volunteers to find those who have experience in training. Then have them conduct the sessions.

83. Mentor Sessions Guide Volunteers

Having volunteers complete a mentor session can round out training and set volunteers on a long-term path for continued growth at your organization.

At the Atlanta Humane Society (Atlanta, GA), nearly 600 volunteers have undergone special training. Volunteers are educated on the history of the nonprofit, the mission statement of the organization, animal handling and customer service.

In addition to attending two-and-a-half hours of training, volunteers wishing to work directly with pet adoptions and pet-facilitated therapy are required to complete a mentor session to complete their training, says Ashley Vitez, volunteer services manager.

This 150-minute mentor session allows a newly trained volunteer to follow a seasoned volunteer giving them a birds-eye view of their responsibilities.

"The mentor shows them where supplies are, how to do an adoption or takes them out in the community to show them what happens on a pet-facilitated therapy visit," says Vitez. "We have found it has helped volunteer retention, because it can be an intimidating or overwhelming experience coming into a shelter, and this gives them another chance to connect with other volunteers and feel more comfortable."

Vitez recommends the following tips for implementing mentoring sessions at your facility:
- ❏ Have a knowledgeable and friendly volunteer conduct the mentoring to make the new volunteers feel welcome and solidify their knowledge learned in training.
- ❏ Consider only offering mentoring on weekends or your nonprofit's busiest time, so new volunteers have plenty of examples from which to learn.
- ❏ Follow up with your new volunteers after the mentoring sessions to ensure they feel comfortable in their new roles and that all critical items were covered with their mentors.

Source: Ashley Vitez, Volunteer Services Manager, Atlanta Humane Society, Atlanta, GA. E-mail: volunteer@atlantahumane.org

Requiring new volunteers to shadow veteran volunteers ensures they will learn what's expected and give them the confidence to carry out their work.

86 Ways to Build Long-term Relationships With New Recruits

84. New Volunteers Deserve Basic Tools

If you're welcoming someone new to your volunteer group, chances are you're not alone. New volunteers are getting involved with projects of all types and commitment levels every day. With that being the case, here's what new volunteers have the right to expect if you want them to perform to their best ability:

1. A thorough orientation procedure.
2. A written job description and sufficient printed materials to help the volunteer learn more about the organization he/she will represent and its programs.
3. Adequate staff support, materials and a work environment that allows the volunteer to do his/her best.
4. Proper recognition and opportunities for growth and development.

If any of these ingredients are missing, it is in the best interest of both the volunteer and the organization he/she represents to see that they are addressed. Doing so will result in a more fulfilling, accomplished experience.

Just as you have certain expectations of new volunteers, it's only right that they have certain expectations met as well.

85. Holiday Volunteer Description Details Role, Responsibilities

Recruiting volunteers over the holidays can be a challenging proposition. But spelling out a role's expected duties and requirements can help potential volunteers better manage their time during this busy season, and save the nonprofit numerous headaches.

Staff at Little Brothers-Friends of the Elderly (Omaha, NE) do this by describing the roles, expectations and details of holiday-specific volunteering positions in one concise form, which is distributed to potential volunteers. Monica Mora-Handlos, volunteer services coordinator, describes how this form has become instrumental in recruiting holiday volunteers:

How is this form used and how is it useful in obtaining volunteers?

"This form (shown right) is available on our website in the volunteer section. When volunteers give of their time, they want to know what will be expected of them, how much time they will need to invest and feel confidence in the organization they will be assisting. The volunteer description form provides potential volunteers with the purpose, the key responsibilities, location, time commitment, volunteer requirements and the benefits of volunteering for that opportunity."

How many additional holiday volunteers do you need to recruit each year?

"Little Brothers-Friends of the Elderly celebrates at least three holidays with our Old Friends including Easter, Thanksgiving and Christmas. We usually need to recruit a minimum of 50 new volunteers each year to assist with our holiday programs."

What tips could you share about creating a form such as this?

"It is vital for agencies to take the time to define each of their volunteer opportunities. It sends a message to volunteers that you believe their volunteer position is as important as a paid office position, when they read a job description for the volunteer opportunities. It also assists the agency to have realistic expectations for volunteers within a position and to be prepared ahead of the volunteer event."

Source: Monica Mora-Handlos, Volunteer Services Coordinator, Little Brothers-Friends of the Elderly, Omaha, NE.
E-mail: mmorahandlos.oma@littlebrothers.org

Content not available in this edition

Nurturing New Volunteers

86 Ways to Build Long-term Relationships With New Recruits

86. Advisory Council Directs, Advocates for Volunteer Program

A volunteer advisory council can help to lookout for the interests of your new recruits and ensure they're getting the attention they deserve.

Creating a volunteer advisory council at your nonprofit can offer your volunteer department the advocacy and direction needed to maintain a strong volunteer force. At the Seattle Cancer Care Alliance (Seattle, WA), dedicated supporters serve two-year terms on an 18-member volunteer advisory council tasked with helping shape the scope of the volunteer services division.

Members of the volunteer advisory council, which is approaching its 20th anniversary, are elected annually. Leadership positions include a president; vice president, who also chairs the development committee; event chairperson; and newsletter chairperson.

"The key to our council is that it is an active and working council," says Erica Karlovits, volunteer services manager. "It's imperative to get people who will be active and can dedicate the time to the council."

Among the council's duties are assisting with volunteer communication and education, as well as developing effective in-services and orientations. It facilitates volunteer preparation for accreditation surveys by conducting monthly mock surveys to offer feedback to staff to ensure information in orientation is being absorbed. It also administers volunteer satisfaction surveys every two years.

The events committee, a segment of the advisory council, provides social events for patients and families. It also orients and recruits new members to the council, and works to educate and develop new leaders throughout the program.

"We try to have our council be as representative of our overall volunteer population as possible, so we attempt to incorporate age diversity as well as gender, cultural and role diversity throughout the council," says Karlovits.

Volunteers serving on the council must have volunteered for a minimum of one year. However, if a new program area is developed, exceptions are made to bring on representatives from new program areas, allowing each segment of volunteer services to have a voice on the advisory council.

"Members of the council are the champions of our programs. We make sure they know the leadership of our program well, which helps us to gain support for the volunteer program," says Karlovits.

"The council is apprised of financial reporting, so they're fully aware of impacts to the department, and we rely on them to advise us on all facets of volunteer services. They are huge stakeholders in our volunteer department."

Source: Erica Karlovits, Manager of Volunteer Services, Seattle Cancer Care Alliance, Seattle, WA. E-mail: ekarlovi@seattlecca.org

Bylaws Help Govern Council

If your organization is considering adding a leadership council to your volunteer organization, create bylaws that will help govern this representative model of volunteer leadership.

When developing the bylaws for your newly formed volunteer advisory council, take a lesson from the Seattle Cancer Care Alliance (Seattle, WA), and add some or all of the following sections to your bylaws:

- Purpose of the council
- Definitions and working terms
- Scope of authority
- Meetings details
- Officers
- Membership
- Resignation and removal procedures

Lightning Source UK Ltd.
Milton Keynes UK
UKOW01f0505030813

214783UK00012B/155/P